T0131564

His Eye Is On The Sparrow

Inspirational Stories of Real Life Miracles

CHARIS CHUNG

BALBOA.PRESS
A DIVISION OF HAY HOUSE

Balboa Press books may be ordered through booksellers or by contacting:

Balboa Press
A Division of Hay House
1663 Liberty Drive
Bloomington, IN 47403
www.balboapress.com
844-682-1282

Because of the dynamic nature of the Internet, any web addresses or
links contained in this book may have changed since publication and
may no longer be valid. The views expressed in this work are solely those
of the author and do not necessarily reflect the views of the publisher,
and the publisher hereby disclaims any responsibility for them.

The author of this book does not dispense medical advice or prescribe the use
of any technique as a form of treatment for physical, emotional, or medical
problems without the advice of a physician, either directly or indirectly. The
intent of the author is only to offer information of a general nature to help
you in your quest for emotional and spiritual well-being. In the event you use
any of the information in this book for yourself, which is your constitutional
right, the author and the publisher assume no responsibility for your actions.

Any people depicted in stock imagery provided by Getty Images are
models, and such images are being used for illustrative purposes only.
Certain stock imagery © Getty Images.

Print information available on the last page.

ISBN: 978-1-9822-7770-3 (sc)
ISBN: 978-1-9822-7772-7 (hc)
ISBN: 978-1-9822-7771-0 (e)

Library of Congress Control Number: 2021924060

Balboa Press rev. date: 01/28/2022

This book is dedicated to my Heavenly Father, my Saviour Jesus Christ, and The Holy Spirit. Without God's grace, Jesus' salvation, and the help from The Holy Spirit, this book would never have been written.

This book is dedicated to my dear mother, Mrs. Chung Wong Yuen Cheun, who is always very dear to my heart, and who is the best living example in my life that I always thank God for!

This book is also dedicated to you. May this book encourage you wherever you are, comfort you even if you are under a dark cloud, and give you hope. God is a true God, and He cares for you. His eye is on you.

God bless you!

CONTENTS

CONTENTS

ACKNOWLEDGEMENTS

I wish to express my deepest love and appreciation to my dearest mother Mrs. Chung Wong Yuen Cheun, for her endless and unconditional love, support and help since I was born. Thank you for giving me freedom to choose my beliefs and the subjects I chose to study throughout the years. I always feel respected, secure and, at the same time, very much thankful to have such loving and an extraordinary mother in my life. You are always a great example and a heroine in my eyes.

I also want to express my gratitude to my dear uncle, Mr. Calvin Chung. Thank you for trying your best to find me the best schools in both British Hong Kong and in Canada. Since my father died when I was seven, you have been a father figure to me, and your love of dogs, cats, birds and fish has inspired and exposed me to a whole new wonderful world! Thank you.

To my brother and sisters Chris, Wai Yee, Zoe, Christine and Cher. My great memories of growing up together, playing together, singing together are all beautiful to me. Thank you for your support and you voting for my book cover!

To one of my dearest cousins Elaine Chung. Your kindness,

support, encouragement and generosity throughout the years at the right time make this book to become possible. I am always thankful to have you in my life!

To my coaches Dr. Sarah Brown and Dr. Colleen Cowles, who have been helping me to start and finish this book. Thank you for your patience, wisdom, brilliant ideas and encouragement! Thank you for encouraging me at times when I was facing challenges or laziness. Thank you sincerely.

To Mr. Sean Linton, my great editor, who has been so patient, encouraging and helpful throughout this writing process. Without your help, this book would not be here. Thank you sincerely.

To Ms. Christy Day, who shares with me her beautiful artistic gift. Thank you sincerely for designing this beautiful book cover which makes this book become more attractive and meaningful.

To the whole publishing team. Without anyone of you, my book would not be here. Everyone of you is deeply appreciated. I sincerely thank you for all your contributions and hard work to make this book become real.

Last but not least, I sincerely thank all my friends who have encouraged or prayed for me and my book throughout this writing journey. Your support, kindness, love and blessings have warmed my heart and encouraged me to finish this. Thank you sincerely.

You all are angels sent from Heaven to me. May this book become a blessing that flows through your lives with God's grace and sends rewards of love and kindness to all of you.

INTRODUCTION

This book is an inspirational memoir which shares the true, first-hand miracles I experienced in my life: how I was miraculously healed when I was facing the final stage of Tuberculosis that even the doctor could not understand; how I got laid off by the company I worked for, then offered a full-time job miraculously two hours later; and how God used me to bring healing to my supervisor's newborn baby grandson. I will also share with you my "out-of-the-body" experience many years ago when I faced death, and how I even saw a glimpse of Heaven and heard the absolute beautiful music there!

This book is like a "power bowl", a power bowl of God's miracles in my life. If you also want to have miracles happen in your life, this book is for you. I will share with you how you can ask and achieve miracles in your life and live in God's grace and mercies daily.

In this book, I will also share with you about my Best Friend whom I have known since I was in kindergarten in British Hong Kong. I started to believe in this Best Friend when I was seven years old. This book is about this Best Friend and His power and miracles. I will share with you how you can also know this friend, develop a close friendship and relationship with Him, how to also ask and perform miracles in your life, and also bless the others with miracles. If you want to have miracles happen in your life, this book is for you! If you want to live better, and be happier, this book is for you. If you want to improve your circumstances and find more hope and peace in your daily living, this book is also for you. It does not matter who you are, what colour of your skin is, where you are, what you have done, and how much help you need, this book will encourage you, and may also lead you to those "dreams" you are hoping for.

I was born in British Hong Kong. I was an international student there, then became citizen in Canada and I now reside in British Columbia. I was trained as a professional performing artist, singer, specializing in Western Art Song and Opera. And in retrospect, I would say my life is as dramatic as an opera itself. Throughout the years, I have faced death a few times. It is by God's grace and miracles that I am still here today to testify His grace and love to me.

Writing this book has been in my heart for over fourteen years. Since I have always been busy studying, performing, working, teaching, and struggling financially as a musician, performer and music and ESL teacher, I become an expert on procrastination.

This book is divided into eight chapters. In each chapter, I share how God, this Best Friend of mine, cares about all areas of our lives: physical, spiritual, financial, vocational, musical and even performs miracles on my little pet birds. Moreover, at the end of each chapter, I will also list some questions to stimulate your own thinking and evaluations.

Do you know that God cares about every little sparrow? Each one of us is a thousand times more precious and valuable than little sparrows in our Creator's eyes. If He watches over and takes care of the little sparrows, He certainly cares about and will take care of you and me.

At this critical time in human history, many people are facing uncertainties, fear, worries, danger, and even death. I pray and hope that this book will bring some hope and encouragement to you, dear friend. This Best Friend that I have is not just for me, He is for you and for everyone in this world. He is for all nations. He loves and cares about you dearly. I guarantee you, if you also develop friendship with Him, He will give you His peace, hope and miracles to your life, and will also give you an eternal life after death. This Best Friend had once died for you before you were born because He loves you, and He wants to befriend with you. You can find Him in this book.

I thank you sincerely for reading this book. I believe it is not an accident you read this book of miracles, and I also pray that this book will bring you many blessings and miracles into your life.

God loves you and bless you!

Sincerely,
Charis Chung

CHAPTER ONE

His Eye Is On The Sparrow

Happy Birthday to you,
Happy Birthday to you,
Happy Birthday to Dear Friend,
Happy Birthday to you!

Every precious life starts with a beginning and ends with a final breath. In between, is the life-long journey which one creates, walks on, learns, grows, changes, improves, achieves, accomplishes, influences. I once heard that it's not about how you start, it's about how you finish. It doesn't matter when your birthday is, your race, your cultural background, your education, or your profession. Sometimes, it's good to think about your life more seriously and more creatively. Or, create your life with a more fun and relaxed attitude.

Without a doubt, "Happy Birthday" is one of the most popular songs we've learned since childhood. Whether it's on our own birthday, or on the birthdays of our family members', our friends', our schoolmates', co-workers', or complete strangers, we all sing the song with happiness, joy, blessings, and congratulations.

However, as you well kown, life is not always happy and joyous. In fact, it can be very challenging and painful sometimes. Life can be very fragile. But regardless of what we face in life, life is still very precious. Life brings excitement, hope, joy, refreshing ideas and moments. For example, if you have pets or plants, you probably have more sensitive emotions and treasure life, as you enjoy seeing them live safely and see them grow. Imagine a puppy or a kitten being born in front of your eyes, or watching a little baby birdie hatched in front of you - how wonderful and amazingly beautiful!

Have you ever saved a life? A trapped dog, a lost kitten, or even a dead plant? After you saved it, how did you feel? I imagine you would be very happy for the life you saved. Or I should say, she must be very happy that you saved her.

I have had a few experiences of trying to save lives. Some were saved. Unfortunately, some were not. But one thing was for sure, the ones that I tried to save or help are all happy that they can live again. And another thing for sure - I was very happy that I at least tried to save them.

When I was a child, I remember saving a little lost ant - I was playing with my siblings in the backyard of our house. I found a little, brown ant wondering around by herself. She walked back and forth, turned left and right, as if she was trying to tell me she needed help. Thinking I must have been the only one who understood her, I quickly ran into the house and got an empty match box.

I ran back and looked for her. There she was! (It actually might have been another lost ant and not the same one. Ha!) I carefully picked her up, quickly put her into the match box safely and ran home with excitement.

It was getting dark soon, and I needed to go to bed shortly, so I decided to get some bread crumbs for her for dinner. I put it nicely beside her, and she seemed interested. I put the match box on the desk in my bedroom, and said goodnight to my new little friend.

The night was longer then I wished, and the first thing I did the next morning was to hope to say good morning to my little "antie". But to my surprise, she was gone! I was kind of disappointed. That was the first time I started to think about life and where it goes.

The second life I tried to save was a little bit more challenging. It was bigger than an ant, and it was a bit damaged. I was in Grade One, if I remember correctly. One rainy afternoon, while I was watching television together with my grandmother and some of my siblings in the living room, my mother came in, looking surprised. She opened her hands and showed us a little sparrow. I ignored the television program right away. My mom told us that the little baby sparrow dropped from a tree while it was raining heavily outside. Yes, it was raining cats and dogs outside all day, and I thought I would be fall out of the tree too if I were the little sparrow. I immediately ran over to my mom and took a look at it. Yes, that little baby sparrow was tiny, weak, but so lovely that I decided to save her.

For the next two hours or so, I was busy gathering some card-board, writing paper, toilet paper, any papers, really. I searched for a pair of scissors, scotch tape, glue.... whatever could stick all my paper together! I knew I had to hurry because I was trying to save a life. Papers dropped here and there, the scotch tape stuck on my fingers instead of taping the papers together, and the glue was all over the place, including on my cheeks as I was rushing and feeling excited inside. I have never done that before. I had never saved a life. It was such a lovely and adorable baby sparrow. I wanted to save her. My sister Cher came by and watched a little while, then she walked off. She probably thought, "There is no hope." But I was trying my best. That little sparrow's life was so precious and I hurried up.

I made a bird house finally! It was a perfect paper house I built for a little baby sparrow, complete with a roof and a bedroom. Her bed was covered with toilet paper.

The little weak sparrow had not died yet, so I quickly moved her into this new house which I had just built for her. Then I ran into the kitchen and asked for some rice and water, running back and forth to feed that little patient sparrow. She opened her mouth and had a little bit water, and a little bit rice. What a good, little Asian sparrow!

Unfortunately, that poor little sparrow died the next day, and tears ran down my cheeks as I missed her. To this day, I still remember her. Even though she was just a little sparrow, she was and still is very precious in my heart.

I started thinking about life more often since then. Life is very short. Life is very fragile. Life is unpredictable. Moreover, I also like thinking about life: Why am I here? Where I am from? How can I come? What should I do in life? What is life about? What will I do in life? How long is my life? What should I do in life?

Since kindergarten, I had learned that there is a God who created me. I started to become a bit more philosophical compared to the same age children I think.

Throughout the years, I had a few other opportunities to save different little lives. Some got saved and some did not. When the life was saved, I was very happy and thankful. And when the life was not saved, besides feeling disappointed, sad, and helpless, every time I could still find God's comfort and a lesson in the experience. Among all of them, the most memorable and successful saving mission happened about six years ago.

The summer of 2014 was one of the hardest summers I've ever had. I had been going through a very hard time and I lost everything. I even had no place to stay and I was looking for a place to settle. I didn't have a car and so I phoned around and looked around for over thirty places. I was very exhausted. Since I decided to go and explore the world a little bit after my post graduate studies to be a Music Educator at University of British Columbia, I quit all my jobs, packed up all my things to put into a storage room, and off I went for a few months to fulfill one of my dreams - Explore the world in traveling.

I went to many places including Alaska, Australia, Indonesia, Singapore, Hong Kong, Hawaii, Califonia, Boston, San Francisco, Guam, Honolulu, Los Angeles, Mexico, Cabo San Lucas, Puerto Vallarta, Japan, Tokyo, Osaka, Hiroshima, Nagasaki, Kagoshima, China, Shanghai, Beijing, Taiwan, Taipei, and other places that I can't remember the names of.

However, when I came back to town, I had no job, no place to stay, no money, and no nothing. It was a very scary thing to do, for sure. Yet, I was thankful that I could rent a living room from a friend whom I've known since I had arrived to Canada as an international student.

As you could probably imagine, life could be very challenging when you are renting and living under the same roof as your landlady. One day, my other former landlady, whom I called Auntie H., who used to rent her room to me in her house in Kitsilano area in Vancouver over the past seven years, invited me to move in with her again in Burnaby. I felt so hopeful that I decided to quickly move one of my two bags into her house one day shortly after. However, the next morning, before I planned to carry my second and last luggage into her house, she phoned me early in the morning unexpectedly while I was sleeping. Suddenly, her whole attitude and voice tone had changed. She yelled at me nonstop on the phone and told me to take away my luggage that I stored in her house the day before. She never gave me any reasons, even though I kept asking why. She felt like a complete stranger, full of cruelty and nonsense, her hostile voice and her yelling echoing in my ears. I was mad that morning but nicely promised that I would be there as soon as possible to pick up my belongings. One thing I did right was, I tell her very nicely and kindly, "Auntie H., it's all fine if you decided not to rent your room to me, but you don't need to be yelling so loudly. I'm not the type of person you assume I am. I can just look for another place. Thank you. I will be there soon." I hung up immediately and sat there on my sofa bed for a while. I had nothing to say. Tears ran down my cheeks. But I realized I didn't need to dwell on these negative emotions. I quickly got up, washed myself and went quickly to pick up all my belongings from her house. I greeted her, quickly went in and picked up my luggage, then walked boldly, with dignity, without turning my head back.

That Sunday summer morning in August was cloudy and a little bit windy. I was still renting that living room from my longtime friend in North Vancouver, but was also trying to phone around and looked for a new place to rent for myself. I went to Lonsdale Quay Market where I go every morning with my Bible, my note book, and my earnest heart, to ask God to help, guide, and provide for me. My routine on those days was to, first go to the Golden "M" Restaurant to get the best deal of the day - the Egg Muffin Meal with my favourite iced coffee. Then I would walk to the Quay and get a good seat outside so I could see the water and breathe in some fresh air.

A few seagulls would come and go every morning, but for the most part, it was a quiet morning that day. After breakfast, I had a conversation with a lady on the phone who was trying to rent out her suite in Vancouver Lower Mainland where I used to live for many years. Yes, Vancouver and North Vancouver are two different cities. If you want to get a job, Vancouver is a better chance, but if you are retired and want to just chit chat with people, then North Vancouver is a better fit.

While I was asking the landlady on the phone if she had a washing machine and dryer at her place, and was also trying to make an appointment to see her place on the phone, all of a sudden, I heard a loud, solid thump on the ground. It didn't sound good. I looked up into the tree, which stood right beside my table. I looked down, and underneath the table, I saw a little sparrow laid down on her back. She was not moving. She was very quiet and not even struggling. I quickly told the lady I had some emergency and had to hang up right away but promised her I would call her back.

I quickly kneeled down and tried to reach the little sparrow, but I couldn't remove the two chairs on my sides and crawled down, using my left hand to grab her.

She was a beautiful, little baby sparrow. I kept asking her how was she doing. I used my left hand to hold onto her and used my right hand index finger to pat her little head. I told her to not be afraid because God loves her. I told her God's eye is on her and God will take care of her. I told her that she is beautiful. I told her almost everything God has told me.

Her eyes were opening and closing slowly and I thought that she would be dying soon. No doubt. So I said to her she would go to Heaven and she would see God. I started to sing to her, I gave her a kiss, and kept patting her little head with my finger. I said a prayer for this beautiful little sparrow and asked God to bless this adorable bird. After about four minutes, all of a sudden, she moved her very weak body and she pooped on my hand. I was surprised, obviously, but I was happy that she had gained her body strength back.

I blessed her by releasing my left hand slowly and said to her, "God bless you!" That beautiful, lovely little sparrow opened up her wings, flew away higher than I thought she could towards the blue skies. I noticed that the weather had already cleared up for her and maybe for me, too. She flew away with great hope, with energy, with all her strength, as if she once again found her life and purpose clearly again. She flew up high towards the skies with victory. Victory over her weakness, victory over her danger, victory over her darkness....

I sat there alone with surprise, somehow comforted with a joyful and thankful heart because God proved to me that His eye is on the sparrow, but also on me. Tears filled my eyes and I kept looking at a photo of her that I had taken on my phone. This precious photo had been shared on my Facebook, kept on my iPhone and sealed on my heart for over six years now. The picture keeps reminding me to trust that God will also take care of me wherever I am.

God's eye is on the sparrow,
And I know He watches me.
His eye is also on you,
For I know He also loves you.

You are very precious in God's eyes. It doesn't matter where you are, or, where you've been dropped. He can always pick you up, kiss you, bless you, and gives you back your life and your spirit, so you can also fly up high again, as you understand your purpose, as you enjoy Him in this world and fill your life with new hope and purpose.

You may ask, "Well, it's good that you saved that little sparrow. But what about my dog that died in a car accident suddenly? Or my kitten that got lost and never returned? Or even my hamster that only lasted for a few months and died on its' wheel? Does God care about my little animals?"

First, I am very sorry for your losses. I also have to say, I don't have all answers for this world. In fact, no one does. But I hope the following miraculous true stories I sincerely share with you in this book will prove that God does care. Yes, even for little animals.

On February 5, 2000, it was the Lunar New Year Day. After talking to my mother overseas in Hong Kong and wishing her a prosperous New Year and her dreams to come true, I thought, Wishing dreams come true? What about my dreams? Is there any dream I would like to fulfill this year? All of a sudden, I remembered I liked little birds when I was a child. My family used to have a German Shepherd, two Basset Hounds, two Lakeland Terriers. We also had different cats, fish and birds at home. Yeah, you can see that I love animals. All of them. But at this point in my life, I figured I could probably only afford birds, so I thought maybe I could make my dream become true that day, too.

And so, I, all of a sudden, decided to go to a pet store and get a little bird for myself. I ended up 'doubling' my dream because I got two little birds. The funny thing is, since they were put together into the same cage at the pet store, I thought they were the same kind of bird. However, I found out one is a Zebra Finch and the other is a Society Finch.

Zebra was a male with a very beautiful orange beak, bright orange cheeks and feet, little polka dots on the side, and a black and white zebra tail. I thought, he was like a buffet dinner - you got everything! I named him Zebra. Brownie was the brownish, female Society Finch which I could only describe as, well, being brown. I used to think that since, I paid forty dollars for them both, and I figured Zebra cost thirty and Brownie cost ten because of the colour. But I adored both of them!

As an ESL instructor at a college myself, I now realize it probably took time for them to communicate and speak to each other. Honestly, they got along very well with each other. I was so happy, excited and thankful that I finally had two little pet birds myself. I had two real lives in my hands and I took it serious. I made sure they ate well, slept well, and were happy.

I have to say, I had a special bond with Zebra, though. I also loved Brownie a lot. Gradually, I noticed Brownie was actually older than Zebra. I could distinguish it by her feet and by her energy compared to Zebra. After about four and a half years, Brownie finally died one day. Both Zebra and I were so heartbroken. That day, I cried for a long time because I missed Brownie. And for Zebra, he never left Brownie's side. He sat next to Brownie in the nest, used his little orange beak to pat Brownie's head for hours. He didn't leave Brownie in the nest.

In the end, I buried Brownie in the backyard of the apartment. Zebra slept alone that night, and I prayed for him. He didn't eat that day or the next. Zebra looked so lonely by himself the next day, and the next few days. Suddenly, a bright new idea came onto my mind: I was going to get Zebra a new girlfriend.

I brought Mi Mi home a few days after Brownie died. Zebra and Mi Mi got along very well with each other because they both were Zebra Finches, and I could tell Zebra liked Mi Mi a lot. They were happy together. And through sincere and continuous prayers, Zebra and Mi Mi then had two lovely baby birdies Tse Tse and Dee Dee! And I was so thrilled by how God answered my prayers.

Zebra and I had a special bond. He trusted me. There were at least three times when I went away on vacation, and the birds were kept at Dr. McDonald's clinic. When I returned, Dr. McDonald told me that after I had been gone for a few days, Zebra was not well. He looked sick and he did not eat much. After doing some tests, Dr. McDonald still could not find anything wrong with him, but she told me to pay attention to Zebra when I took him back home and to see if he had anything wrong. But every time after I took him home, he was happy, hopping here and there and chirping again. In the end, Dr. McDonald and I both agreed that it was because Zebra missed me very much when I was away.

God performed miracles on Zebra a few times. But one significant healing He performed on Zebra was very impressive. Zebra was sick with a liver problem and he stayed at the hospital at Dr. McDonald's for a few days.

That was a Sunday. Right after the Sunday service at church, when the prayer leaders were standing in front of the pulpit, and told us if we need any prayers, we could go up and request prayers for anything. I quickly walked up, not only because I believe in prayers, but I also wanted to pray for little Zebra.

Sabina was one of the senior prayer leaders at the Church, as well as a retired nurse. I have known Sabina for many years and she and her husband Jack have always been my mentors. They are without a doubt some of the most highly respected people I've ever encountered in life. Sabina is one of the most gentle and loving people that I've known. Moreover, one very special thing about Sabina is, sometimes when she prays, she can hear God's voice or see pictures. She told me she has had that gift since she was little.

That day after church, I ran up to Sabina because I wanted to pray for Zebra desperately. After listening to Zebra's condition, Sabina said she would pray and see if there was anything she could hear. Right away after about two seconds, she told me she saw Jesus, and He was holding my little bird. She also saw that Jesus gave my little bird a kiss. Somehow, I felt comforted by what she told me. I sensed that Jesus was going to heal my little Zebra. I also noticed that there was a line of people waiting for Sabina's prayers and blessings. I thanked her, gave her a hug, said goodbye, and left that Sunday service with hope and peace in my heart.

That same night around seven o'clock in the evening, my phone rang, and I was surprised to know that it was Dr. McDonald. I have known Dr. McDonald for years but she had never called me at home. That night, she called and I thought it must be about Zebra. I answered the phone with a bit of nervousness. My heart pounded when I heard Dr. McDonald say, "I want to let you know that I don't know why, but today around 12:30pm, all of a sudden, Zebra was feeling much better. He started to eat and I checked on him, and found he is much better now. So, if you'd like, you can come tomorrow and take him home."

I hung up the phone and started dancing and singing and praising God in my living room. And when I thought back around 12:30pm? That was exactly the same time I asked Sabina to pray for my little Zebra! And I knew God's eye was definitely on His loved ones. Even for a little finch like Zebra. That was the last time God healed Zebra physically because one full year later, when Zebra was almost eight years old, on January 20, 2008, one week after my birthday, Zebra died in my palm.

Look at the birds of the air,
For they do not sow, nor reap,
Nor gather crops into barns,
And yet your heavenly Father feeds them.
Are you not much more important than they?

Matthew 6:26

Every one of us is precious. Precious in the eyes of our loved ones' and precious in God's eyes especially. No one of us are the same. Each one of us is special, unique, and created in a significant way by the Creator of this world and the God of this universe. Whether we are black or white, boys or girls, young or old, we are all here on earth for a purpose, for a reason, and for a "mission". We may be born in different countries, speak different languages, and have different outlook and born with different characters and personalities, but we've all come for a purpose, a reason, and a meaning. Just like that little sparrow I saved at Lonsdale Quay, she was born to fly, to sing, to give us freshness and a beautiful song each day. She was precious in God's view, and that is why I believe why God saved her. In her danger, God used me to pick her up, to give her hope and to comfort her, and in the end, God healed and saved her. She flew up high again and carried on her life journey with boldness, with experience, and with braveness.

A bird's life is fragile. However, do you know that a human's life can also be very fragile, too? I am living today, but it does not mean that I am guaranteed that I will be living tomorrow. Like that little ant and the little baby sparrow I tried to save, they both disappeared and died on the next day. Life is short, and it is wise to treasure our fragile lives.

14

We all can live and "fly" like that little sparrow to carry on with our life journey, regardless of where we are in our lives or in our situations. As the little sparrow, I also wish for God to inspire me and this book to give you hope, to encourage you, to give you new insights and to bring you new blessings.

QUESTIONS TO EXPLORE:

Q. 1 When have you experienced life is fragile?

Q. 2 Have you ever experienced a Miracle in your life in a fragile situation?

Q. 3 When looking back in life, can you see God's Hands to help you in a special situation?

CHAPTER TWO

God's Eye Is On Friendship

**There is one friend I know,
Who has known me before I was molded.
This friend reveals his grace to me when I grow.
I spend time and water this friendship
with what I was told.
When challenges and darkness come to take hold,
I see this friend protect me wherever I go.**

Charis Chung

We all have friends and need good friends. We need friends who share their help when we are in need. We need friends who build us up and not tear us down. We need friends who listen and understand us, who also stay with us when all others walk away. I know it's hard to have good friends. Thus, if you have good friends to help, support, and love you, and who are always on your side, you need to be very thankful.

Here I want to introduce you my best friend. A very

special friend who knew me before I was born. A friend who is powerful but humble. A friend who has unlimited resources and who is always willing to help whenever I ask him for help. When I was first introduced to this friend, I did not know his love is so real; his power is so miraculous; his grace is so true; and his help is so practical.

In the following chapters, I will share some miracles that this friend has performed in my life so you can understand his true power and love. But for now, I'd like to share how I came to know this friend and how the friendship developed. Moreover, throughout the years, when I faced challenges, non-curable sickness, difficulties, loosing my jobs, this true friend extended his hand, his help, his love, his grace, and his miracles to me again and again. This friend is real, and he is still living in our midst in this world today. I sincerely hope you also will know this friend and develop an intimate friendship with him.

I was born in British, Hong Kong. During my childhood, I enjoyed a safe and protected environment under the British Government. I enjoyed freedom of speech, freedom of act, and freedom of choice, similar to my life here in Canada. In retrospect, I am very thankful for the safe and respectful environment I grow up from.

Compared to many of my young friends I knew in my childhood, I would say, me and my family were one of the "fortunate" ones who lived in British, Hong Kong that time. This is because we used to live in a good house, which always came with a backyard or we called a "garden". We had different puppies, kittens, fish, birds as pets and we also had fruit trees like papaya trees and lai chi trees. I would say that, we lived in a very comfortable environment. I'm always thankful for this big blessing for a small child.

When I was in kindergarten, my favourite pastime was reading and listening to the Bible stories. I think it was wise for me to believe that there was a God who created this world. It was important for me to believe God loved people, since He gave me life so I could go to school and listen to His stories every day. I was comforting to know that He forgives us when we sin or do something wrong. I used to like stealing candies, and every time I did, I felt, guilty. But when I confessed to my mother, she always forgave me.

And I realized that God is kind and forgiving like my mother. So since I was in kindergarten, I believed, and still believe in God.

Immaculate Heart of Mary School is my favourite Elementary School. I am always thankful that my Uncle Calvin found this fantastic school for us after my father died. I studied there from grade two to grade six.

I remember in grade two, when I was seven-years-old (the same year my father died suddenly) I believed in God and I accepted Jesus Christ into my heart. I believed all the true stories I read from the Bible, and I also believed Jesus Christ is the Son of God, like my brother Chris is the son of my father. I believed Jesus died on the cross for all of our sins, including the sin of stealing all the candies from home. I also believed that every time I would admit my sins and confess, God would forgive me.

I did not go to church until I was in high school, when I was studying at a Buddhist secondary school. The more

I learned how fragile one's life is from the Buddhist's philosophy, the more I thought about going to church and learning about God Himself. Life is short, after all. This concept of going to church to know more about God had been on my mind for about a year and a half. Finally, I begged my high school buddy May Ying to go to a Catholic church with me after school. I chose a Catholic church first it was because of my history at the Immaculate Heart of Mary School. I remember every Thursday after school, me and May Ying would go to the church and had the Bible studies with the father at the church, where we learned about God, His words, His teachings and His salvation to all human kind.

During the year I attended the Catholic church, there were a few things I felt a little bit uncomfortable about. So after one year, I decided to try to attend an Evangelical Christian church one Sunday.

Once I arrived the Christian church, I right away felt myself so much closer to God. At the same time, I felt it was also much easier and simpler to talk to God at any time. Since then, I never stopped attending church.

I accepted Jesus Christ again (the second time after my kindergarten year) and I was baptized before I came to Canada as an international student. I like spending time with God since I started attending church.

After I finished high school, I decided to tutor students at home so I could have more private time to spend with God and to have a more free schedule. I remember, every morning I got up early. After breakfast, I would spend at least one and a half to two hours with God, praising Him, singing songs, reading the Bible, and praying to Him. I would write down notes and prayer items on my Bible study journal. I also kept an eye on all the answered prayers by God. I could say that, I started and developed a pretty healthy routine, as well as a friendship and relationship with God, and God blessed me with a good foundation in our 'friendship'.

As I said earlier, my friendship with God started when I was little. It carried on throughout my teenager years, and when I came by myself to Canada as an international student, I always kept to myself to have close friendship with God. Wherever I live, I always find a church (or even two) to attend, to serve, and to have fellowship with some good Christian friends.

However, one thing I learned - do not look at the people at church. Look at God Himself. People can drag and tear you down, but God always builds you up. People are sinful, but God is holy. People may always like to get from what you have, but God always tries to give and bless you what you need. What a friend we can have in God!

I learned that time is one of the most important elements to develop a solid, good friendship and relationship. My friendship with God works the same way. I spend time with God. I spend time listening to God's words from different ministries like the Turning Point Ministry with Dr. David Jeremiah; the Daily Hope with Dr. Rick Warren; the Blessed Life with Dr. Robert Morris; the Healing Journey and Tipping Point Ministry with Dr. Jimmy Evans; and many other spiritual "giants" like Adrian Rogers and Jentezen Franklin. I like reading devotional books and I also like to spend time in prayer. I plan personal retreats or fast and pray once in a while in order to focus more time on spending moments with God and worshipping Him.

There were a few times, instead of staying in jobs where I could earn more money but felt exhausted, spiritually and mentally, I chose to change to jobs which were less stressful. I chose jobs where I could have free time to bring my Bible and note-book in to work and spend time with God alone when there was no students came in. (With the permission from my supervisors, of course.) The thing is, I found all the time I spent with God was not wasted because I build a solid, strong, and wonderful friendship that money could never buy. Moreover, to my surprise, I found God Himself treats me as His friend! He directs me, listens to my prayers, answers my prayers, and performs His miracles with me again and again, which always amazed me.

God always wants to befriend with you, too. If you have never been told about this, I want to sincerely tell you: God created you, and you are very precious and valuable in His eyes. Since we were born on earth, we came with all wrong thoughts, the wrong ideas that lead us to wrong doings in our lives. And because God is hundred-percent holy, we could never reach to His holiness and be with Him. In order to reach and save us, God Himself decided to send His only son, Jesus Christ, to be born on earth, (that is why we celebrate Christmas every year), and Jesus died on the cross for all people on earth (and that is why we celebrate Easter every year). He paid the price for our sins, so we can become sinless, because when we accept Jesus Christ as our saviour, we welcome Him into our hearts, and we ask Him to forgive and change us, then the blood of Jesus will wash away all of our sins, as we become clean and sinless. When we have Jesus inside us, God will not see our 'old selves', but a 'new us' inside us with the image of Jesus Christ alongside us, who is sinless. Moreover, once we become a child of God, we can enjoy the friendship and relationship with God on earth right away. Not only that. One day when we die, when we leave this earth, we can go straight to Heaven and be with God eternally! This is a free gift from God to you, dear friend, so would you like to accept Jesus and God's gift to you?

"Behold, I stand at the door and knock.
If anyone hears My voice and opens the door,
I will come in to him and dine with him,
and he with Me."

Revelation 3:20

God's friendship is practical. When God is your friend, you can depend on Him because whenever you call Him, He will always answer. His answers may not to follow everything you ask (otherwise; you will be God), but He answers with love, grace, and mercy according to His will, which is also the best for you.

I just said God's friendship is practical and I mean it. I can also proof it. This is one of the very early miracles I received from God when I came over from British, Hong Kong to British Columbia.

I was an international student studying music at a community college. Long ago, the government laws were very different. We were not allowed to work anywhere. Not at all, only study. And as international students, the Canadian government charged us a fortune. (about four times what the local students' pay) It didn't matter how much you wanted to work and how poor you were, it was illegal for international students to work. After quite a few years, thank God, the government finally changed her laws for all international students - you could only work if you could find a job on the same campus where you studied. That's right, not outside the campus, only on the same campus where you study. I calculated the probability would be about one to one million and thirty thousand of a chance to get a job on the same campus where I studied (just kidding). The only once chance I had in winning was, I thought, if I prayed and asked God. The thing was, how could I get a job? I was an international student and I even knew some of the local students who were born here also looked for jobs. Why would employers hire me but not them? The more I questioned, the more I thought I would never get a job. But I hung on to God. I prayed to Him earnestly to get a job, on campus, so I could earn some money to sustain myself here as I really hoped to lighten my family's burden.

Somehow, the Holy Spirit helped me. I typed up my resume, and I went to the college cafeteria and talked to the manager there. I explained to him that I was sincerely looking for a summer job that I could earn some money for tuitions. The manager listened to me, took my resume, but did not offer me anything and promised nothing. I left the cafeteria but kept praying to God and wished this Friend would help me.

One day, the cafeteria manager called me and asked me to go for an interview. And in the end, he hired me right away to work full time for that whole summer! I was so thankful and happy, counting it as a big blessing, especially since I later found out that I was actually the first and only international student who worked there on the campus.

After I started working there, more and more local and international students came to me and asked why they gave me the job and how they could get a job. The cafeteria job was a very hard summer job because I had to stand for at least eight hours a day for work, cutting and chopping and even sometimes cutting my own fingers. I also had to carry very heavy ice buckets and grilled the burgers which I did not like doing (it was very hard on my vocal chords as I was learning singing at the Music College), but I was very thankful for the special miracle God performed to help me.

But this friend didn't just help out one time.

After studying singing with Dr. Jacob Hamm for about four years, he told me that he had already taught me everything I needed to know, and encouraged me to move on with one of the best voice teachers in British Columbia at the time, Ms. P. Mailing. At the time, Ms. Mailing was the Voice Department Head at the Academy of Music.

But instead of studying with her, I stopped taking any lessons for a while due to my financial situation. Being a music student is already hard enough, but I never had extra money to enjoy any luxury. Even though I had been hoping to contact Ms. Mailing for a while, I would never have the money to pay for my voice lessons, so I thought, why bother?

One Sunday morning when I opened my eyes, a little voice reminded me that I should phone Ms. Mailing and talk to her about my voice lessons. I hesitated because I knew I had no money. But knowing that God sometimes would talk to me when I first opened my eyes in the morning, I started to reconsider. Feeling pretty strongly that it was the Holy

Spirit talked to me, I called the music school and talked to Ms. Mailing on Monday when the school was opened.

I told Ms. Mailing about my former voice teacher Dr. J. Hamm and how he recommended her to me. She did not promise she would teach me on the phone. Instead, she suggested that I go and do an audition for her first. So for the next short while, I worked with my vocal coach, and went to audition for her.

Ms. Mailing seemed to be very happy with me after she heard me sing. She was warm and kind, and she suggested that I register for singing lessons with her at the administrative office.

However, at the end of the audition, she mentioned the price: $1,400 for the year. And this was only for weekly one-hour lessons during the school year. I said to myself, that was even more expensive than my life! I didn't even have one hundred forty dollars in my pocket, how could I get that one thousand four hundred dollars? In fact, I would be moving to a smaller place shortly to share a basement suite with another girl, who was also a student, in order for me to save some money. How could I get $1,400 for my luxury voice lessons? I started to pray to God again because I knew that would be my best chance. I remembered a preacher said that before we pray, we need to be specific about what we are asking for. So I asked,

"Dear Heavenly Father, I have always been hoping to take voice lessons again since I stopped learning from Dr. Hamm. I thank You for such a great teacher I had. I thank You for providing a person like Dr. Hamm for he had not only been a father figure to me in my learning, but he was

25

so kind in helping me get my first CD-player from the States and for buying me two big chocolate bars when I went home to visit. I have now met Ms. Mailing, and she was happy to teach me. But the tuition is very expensive! I just cannot afford it at all. But I know You are a great God! You've always helped me when I am in need. Lord, I do not know where I can get that $1,400 for my tuition. It is impossible for me. But I know You from the past miracles in my life. I know if You are willing to help me, You will have Your way, and I pray that You will help me. God, I really want to take voice lessons again. I hope to take lessons with this new voice teacher, and I pray that You will help me. In Jesus' name I pray. Amen."

My prayer was short and specific, and I repeated a few times every day.

I had just moved into a basement suite, sharing the suite with another girl who was planning to study fashion design. Each of us has our own bedroom, but my things were all over the place. Boxes were everywhere and I was incredibly exhausted. I had been moving so many times that even the secretary at the music college once told me that all my furnitures should have wheels on them so I could move faster. But who wants to move regularly? I had been moving a lot because my financial situation as a musician had never been stable. I had to connect my phone line properly every time before I move into a new place. It was not only for my convenience; but also for safety purposes, in case if there is any emergency situations.

I was so exhausted after moving into that basement suite, and I had been unpacking since the night before, so I lied down for a while on my bed to rest a little bit. Suddenly, the phone rang.

It was a familiar voice asking for me. She said she was K. Kelly, the Director of Human Resources at the music college I used to attend. Of course I remembered Ms. Kelly! When I was a music student there, I used to wait outside different classrooms in the morning, during lunch time or after school in order to get a room to practise once classes finished, and Ms. Kelly often walked past me in the hallways. One day she very kindly to stopped by and talked to me about my studies. Later when I got a job at the Music Department as the Professor's Assistant, Ms. Kelly saw me many times when I went to the Human Resources Department to get help or pick up letters from the department. I was not sure if I was a trouble maker, but there were a few times I showed up in her office.

But why did she call me that afternoon? She told me she was trying to clean up all the files in her office, and my file was on her hand. She said she remembered I used to look for jobs on campus and was wondering if I was still looking for jobs or interested in getting a job. I immediately said yes. At the end of the call, she arranged for me to go for an interview with the Admissions Office Manager the next day, and I got another full time summer job. I counted every pay cheque I got that summer, and at the end, the total amount I got from my job was slightly over $1,400. Thus, I immediately registered into the music academy for the following school year program and studied voice with Ms. Mailing from September to April.

God not only miraculously blessed me with that $1,400 that summer. It was also a miracle that Ms. Kelly remembered me and she called me herself. I was just a no name small potato, so why would she, the Director of the Human Resources Department from a well-known college call me? I could not figure out a better reason besides God's mercies and His kindness to help me.

God's help and His miracles did not stop after that $1,400. Afterwards, God performed miracles again and again throughout the years I was on the campus and even after my jobs there at the college. One thing I believe and have learned that God's miracles require us to also take our steps. In other words, God wants and needs us to participate with Him to perform miracles in our lives. He wants us to work with Him together hand in hand, as a friend, to perform miracles to ourselves and to people around us.

Would you like to know this friend? Are you ready to know more about Him? Do you want to have miracles in your life? Would you like to work hand in hand with Him? Would you also like to perform miracles for people around you and to this world?

**"For God so loved the world
that He gave His only begotten Son,
that whoever believes in Him should not perish
but have everlasting life."**

John 3:16

God has a plan to save us all people in this world. So, He sent Jesus to come on earth to die for all of us so we can have eternal life. But if Jesus was not willing to come to earth, we would not have any salvation from God. In the story I shared with you, the morning when the Holy Spirit told me to phone the music school and take lessons with Ms. Mailing was monumental if I did not take the steps to call in, to audition, I would not have seen the miracles God has prepared for me.

If you have a friend who can share money with you when you are in need, you have a good friend. If you have friends who can pray for you and cook for you when you are sick, you need to be very thankful. If you have friends who can listen to you about your troubles and your difficulties, you should appreciate these friends you have. It is not easy to have good friends. But I can guarantee you, if you accept and take Jesus as your friend, learn about Him, spend time with Him, talk to Him, also allow Him to talk to you, listen to Him, follow Him, obey Him. He can do miracles after miracles in your life.

God's eye is on friendship - the friendship between you and Him. He has been waiting for you to reach out to Him, and He has always been standing at the door, knocking at the door of your heart. Whenever you are ready to open the door and invite Him to be as your friend, He will come in and bless you with all His blessings. But this friendship goes two ways. You also need to spend time with Him, to learn about Him and His love for you and to learn about His character, His commands and His teachings that can change your life. His words and His wisdom can improve your life and set you free on your difficulties. He is the best friend you can find on earth.

QUESTIONS TO EXPLORE:

Q. 1 God has extended His hand to you, would you like to accept His friendship?

Q. 2 God knows everything about you because He created you. Would you also like to know Him?

Q. 3 If you want to accept this friendship from God, how are you going to develop this friendship?

CHAPTER THREE

How You Can Have Miracles in Life

A miracle without a wand,
Is not just to receive what you want.
It is to express how much God loves you to want,
To walk closer and closer to
Him even when you are
in a deep, dark pond.
A miracle from Him will bless
you beyond what you want,
And God wants you to use this 'wand',
To bless people around you wherever
you want or do not want.

Charis Chung

Writing this book has been in my heart for at least fourteen years. Yes, I'm not joking at all here. The idea of writing a book to testify this God, His glory and His miracles has been on my heart for a very long time. Moreover, there were at least eight or nine times that I thought about it seriously, then put it aside.

I've thought about it since the year when I was completely healed by God in the final stage of tuberculosis during my first year studying at a music college. God did a few miracles even the doctor could not understand. God healed my heart condition at one time instantly without medication.

And how God opened doors for me again and again when the others were trying hard to 'slam the door' in my face in the opera school. Again and again, God extended not only His friendship, but also His kindness, His mercies, His comfort, His miracles.

As a poor musician, sustaining myself was already not easy. I have always been running around rehearsing, performing (especially in the past years), studying, working, teaching and serving at different churches. My greatest excuses were focused on having no money and no time. Gradually, I become an expert on procrastination.

But God's grace is always generous. He never yelled at me. Instead, He has always continued reminding me of this 'mission' with a still, small voice. At the same time, throughout the years, He has shown me more and more of His miracles which gives me a handful to share. Thus, I have to say honestly that in this small, little book, I just cannot share all the miracles that God performed for me throughout the years in detail. But I certainly will share a glimpse of His glory and hope to encourage you and give you some hope. I will also share with you how you can also get miracles in your life in this chapter. If you also want to get blessed by God and His miracles, please be patient and I will share with you step by step how you can have miracles in your life and even how to perform miracles to the others with either your loved ones or someone you do not know. God wants to bless you, and He also wants you to be a blessing to the others and the world.

To see and know God's miracles, we have to have a sensitive heart, mind, ears and eyes.

Do you see God's miracles are all around us? The beautiful trees, flowers, mountains, insects, animals, birds, rivers, lakes and oceans all reveal to me how marvelous this God the Creator is! Do you hear God's miracles are around us? The blowing wind, the sound of the raindrops, the singing birds, the crying of the new born babies, the different instruments playing together and the water fountains are all echoing the beauty of the nature and comforting to our souls. They are so real and beautiful!

Are you sensitive to see miracles when someone sends you a thank you note or to see how you are doing? Or when someone gives you a call when you are down? What about the lessons you hear on radio about God loving the world and loving you? What about the beautiful churches around your city, and the people all gathering together to worship? Do they touch your heart or talk to you in a special way?

God's miracles and love are all around us. And if you do not see it or hear it, I suggest you to spend some quiet time, alone by yourself, soaking into nature and closing your eyes, breathing in the fresh air, and feeling like you are actually part of nature. You are part of this universe. And most importantly, you are part of God's kingdom.

God's miracles are not always big and supercalifragilisticexpialidocious. God moves in big moments and He also moves in small little ones.

Do you want to have God's miracles happen in your life? Do you need a miracle? Or do you want to perform a miracle in your loved one's life? If you do, I will share with you what I have learned through the years on how to have God's miracles in your life and how God can also use you to perform miracles to people whom you do not even know!

In order to have God's miracles in our lives, we first need to have a problem or a 'mountain' in front of us that we cannot move. Some situations or disease are beyond what we can control or solve, or it's just too difficult or too hard for us to face. It's in these moments where we can look beyond ourselves and search for a 'higher power'. Here is a true story happened to my friend Stormie.

I knew Stormie for a long time but we had lost contact with each other also for a few years. And during those years, Stormie and her husband had been trying to have a baby struggling. They tried to see different doctors, talked to different counsellors at church, they took different friends' advice and admitted and believed that to remain childless was the plan and the 'fate' God had for them.

One day, after a few years of not seeing each other, Stormie and I bumped into each other on the Skytrain. We caught up on the train, and Stormie eventually told me about their story. Stormie's eyes were with tears when she told me she and her husband believed this is their 'fate' and what God had for them - no baby in their marriage.

I confidently and strongly told Stormie: "I don't believe what your friends, counsellors and pastors told you." Stormie reacted very shocked and puzzled when she looked at me. I asked if her and her husband really wanted to have a baby and she nodded. I told her we can ask God and I am sure God will bless them with a baby. I suggested we pray for the situation in our private time and also suggested we get together once a month for a prayer meeting and pray together for the desires of their hearts. And we did. Stormie and I met once a month for dinner, then went to my apartment suite and prayed for a miracle.

Here, as you can see, the second step to have God's miracles in your life is to go to God and ask and pray. Many people believe in all different religions, saints, philosophers, Buddha, or a god of all sorts. But as I understand, there is only one God who created this world. This One and Only God is the God! This true God is the Creator of this world and universe. This God is the God of Noah who built Noah's Ark. This is also the same God of King David, who was the true King of Israel. This is also the God who created this world in Genesis!

This is also the God who creates you and me! All lives are from God. This true God is three-in-one. To make it simple for you, dear friend, so you can understand easier, think of a triangle: there are three points: A, B and C. God is: the Father, Jesus Christ and the Holy Spirit. Or even simpler: the Father, Son and the Spirit.

In order to have miracles in our lives, we have to find and ask the Only True God, the God Who Created this world and who owns all things, powers and miracles. Otherwise, we are finding the wrong object and the wrong God. And to go to this true God, we need to believe in Him. In other words, we need to have faith in this true God.

What do I believe in this true God? I believe God is the Creator of this world. I believe God also created all human beings and all living things in this world. I believe we are all sinners. We all do something wrong in lives - we jay-walk, we gossip, we lie, we steal candy or we cheat on our quizzes at schools. So we all need God to forgive us. How? To pay for our sins or wrong doings, God sent His son, Jesus Christ, to come to us, to be born on earth and die for us on the cross. But after three days of His death, Jesus Christ rose again. He was resurrected from death. This is why we celebrate Easter.

Jesus Christ shows us if we believe in Him, believe He is the Son of God who came to save us, receive Jesus Christ in our hearts, apologize to Him for our own sins and ask Him to forgive us, His blood on the cross will cleanse us from all our sins, and all of our wrong doings. Only then will we be forgiven for our sins totally and completely. With no more sins in us, we can come to God and ask and pray to Him, like a child goes to his or her loving father, God will listen to us and God will answer our prayers.

Here I want to emphasize that, we do not order God to do what we tell Him to do and ask God to 'obey' us. Otherwise, we would be "God". Instead, we ask and pray with a humble attitude. We have to let God be God. Our part is to tell Him how we feel, what we want or desire, tell Him what happened, what we need, what we hope for, and what we wish, but not order or manipulate Him. To make it clear and simple we tell Him the best and let God do the rest. And if we keep a positive mind and have gratitude no matter what the outcome is, believing He is the best Father, He will do the best for us, regardless of how we see the final outcome.

> **"Ask, and it will be given to you;**
> **Seek, and you will find;**
> **Knock, and it will be opened to you.**
> **For everyone who asks receives,**
> **And he who seeks finds,**
> **And to him who knocks it will be opened.**
> **Or what man is there among you who,**
> **If his son asks for bread,**
> **Will give him a stone?**
> **Or if he asks for a fish,**
> **Will he give him a serpent?**
> **If you then, being evil,**
> **Know how to give good gifts to your children,**
> **How much more will your Father who is in heaven**
> **Give good things to those who ask Him!"**

Matthew 7:7 - 11

There are few things I would like to share with you that you may want to pay attention to when praying. I learned that a good prayer should consist of five parts:

1. **Praise and Adoration.** First, spend some time praising who God is. Praise His holiness, His power, His grace, His love for this world and for us, His creation. Express to God how marvelous He is, and express to God how much you adore and appreciate Him as your Heavenly Father and for His love for human beings and for yourself.

2. **Thanksgiving.** Thank God for His love to you. You may want to thank God for your family, your siblings, your friends, your job, your blessings, your day off, your vacation, and your financial abundance. Just count your blessings and thank Him sincerely. You may even want to thank Him for reading this little book! Thank God for your cleverness and intelligence in understanding what I am sharing here. This is also a very important part of a good prayer.

3. **Intercessions.** This is the part where you pray for the others. It can be your parents, your family, your friends, your co-workers, your boss, your pet dogs and cats, or even your enemies! A good prayer will never be just praying for yourself. It has to include people, things, or situations around us. Do not be afraid to pour out your heart to talk to God. He is a compassionate God and He is more than happy to hear from you regarding all the things that are on your heart. He does not sleep or slumber, and you can talk to Him 24/7.

4. **Petition.** This is the part of prayer that you ask God for your own needs. For example; you can ask God for your financial needs, your spiritual needs and understanding, your career directions and blessings, your emotional needs and healing, or your desire for Him to help you in any difficult situation. Or you can even ask God to help you understand who He is and ask God to give you faith and hope and a close friendship with Him! Once again, God loves to hear from you, so do not be hesitate to talk to Him in details about your situations and concerns.

5. Confession. This is the part where we admit our wrong doings and ask God to forgive us. Everyone in the world is a sinner, and whoever comes to God and ask for forgiveness, will be forgiven. I personally like to put this step right after I praise God. It is because I like the idea to have a clean and pure heart first before I ask for my needs or others' needs. I somehow feel it is more pleasing to God if I come with a clean and pure heart. Moreover, when there are no sins between me and God after I confess all my sins and 'dirt', God can even see me and hear me more clearly.

When my friend Stormie and I met once a month to pray together, we basically followed the same cycle - we spent a few minutes praising how great our God is first, then we usually thanked God for taking care of us for the past month, and we thanked Him also for special blessings we received. Afterwards, we prayed for the other's needs and concerns before we pray for our own problems or situations. We also would pray for our friends' or our family's needs and situations. Then we would also pray for ourselves because we always knew our situations and difficulties better than the others. And of course; we always confess our sins and ask God to forgive us so we could have a clean and pure heart and mind to worship and adore Him. We kept praying every time we met. God sometimes answered our prayers pretty quickly, but sometimes some of the prayers took a longer time. No doubt about it. But do not loose hope as this is exactly what the evil spirit wants you to do to give up.

After we spent a few months praying for Stormie and her husband to have a baby, there were a few things happened that caught our attention. First, Stormie told me that God talked to both of them individually in their own private time about adopting a baby. Both of them were very surprised when they talked to each other about the idea and the same desire. Then Stormie and I started to pray for the application, the different interviews and meetings, and later about the process and procedures, and buying plane tickets for them to fly to foreign country to pick up the baby God had blessed them with an adopted child! But since Stormie told me they both wish to have their own biological baby, we kept on praying each month together.

Another several months passed. One day when I found out there was going to have a healing service in Richmond, B.C., I told Stormie to go there with her husband. I encouraged them not to be afraid to go and ask the pastors to pray for them and their situation. I encouraged them to go for the healing service because years earlier, I myself went to that service and God completely healed my back pain.

One late night around 11:50pm, Stormie phoned me and apologized for calling me very late. Her voice was excited and she told me what happened during the healing service earlier that night. In short, she told me they both went out and asked for healing and a blessing during the service. Surprisingly, the pastor (who do not know them at all) told them that God knew they had lost a baby before but God would bless them with two babies, and one would be their own biological child. I have never seen Stormie be so excited before, and deep in my heart, I knew God would bless them with their baby soon, and I was very happy for them!

Then another several months passed by, and we continued meeting and praying and in the end we finally were astonished by the good news about Stormie's pregnancy. The beautiful baby boy was born several months afterwards in the summer.

Prayers evade the impossibilities, and in the name of Jesus Christ, the Son of God, all things are possible. Praise The Lord! In my opinion, we first need to confess our sins, then receive Jesus Christ as the Son of God and as our Saviour. (Jesus is like the bridge between God and us. By believing in Jesus, we can go back to God Himself.) When we become the children of God, we can then go to God at any time to express our feelings, our wishes, our hearts, and God will answer us according to His grace and love to us with His power and sovereignty. Here I would like to emphasize, God has sovereignty in His authority to say Yes or no, or to have us wait for the answers to our prayers. Our job is to express ourselves to Him, to talk to Him, and to leave all things in God's hands, knowing and trusting that God knows what is best for us and plans accordingly. He is our perfect Father, and He is God Himself.

I also want to share that it is crucial to spend time with one another, creating fellowship among friends and with God, as we ask and pray for miracles. When friendships consist of believers together, we become stronger, we grow our faith together in God, and we encourage each other, building each other up to create a positive and strong faith, mind and thinking in God. The time we spend with brothers and sisters in prayer will never be wasted, since God said in His Bible that when two or three get together in prayers, God will listen and answer us. Moreover, when we are together, to spend time and to share with each other, it helps us to eliminate all negative thoughts, fears, and anxieties from our minds and replace them with love, joy, peace, strength and positive thoughts and strength into our mind and soul.

In order to see the changes in our situations and to see the miracles, we have to change our inner self first.

Just like when I would get together with Stormie, we used to go for a nice dinner to spend time chatting, laughing, and sharing good food with each other first. Then when we would get together in my apartment suite to pray, we'd read some Bible verses or, sing a song, and we'd share our prayers with each other to warm up, and then we'd pray together. Afterwards, we would sometimes have tea together. I believe that, every moment we spent together, God was there and He was listening and blessing us all the way through.

To have miracles in our lives, we need to pray consistently. When I am praying for a miracle, sometimes I pray at least ten times a day for the miracle. And I pray whenever and wherever. I say long prayers and I also say conversational prayers which are short prayers at any moment. I set time aside to pray for the specific miracle. Sometimes I go for a prayer walk by myself. Sometimes I pray throughout the day. And sometimes I set aside time on the weekend to pray for specific things. And when the Holy Spirit directs, I may also fast and pray. I try to attend church prayer meetings or some individual prayer sessions. In short, pray as much as you can because no prayers will ever be wasted!

I also want to encourage you here, read the Bible and use the Bible to pray. As I said earlier, get a Bible from any bookstore and start reading since the Bible is God's holy words and love letter to all people on earth. Do you know that according to the Guinness World Records, the Bible is the most popular and the most read book in the world? People read other books, but the Bible reads you. The Bible tells you who you are, where you belong, and where you will go.

However, it is impossible to read all books from the Bible at one time. I suggest to start reading the Gospel of John in the New Testament, the book of Psalm, and the book of Proverbs in the Old Testament every day. Find a good quiet place at home, by yourself, and may be spend about twenty minutes each day to start with. It will be a blessing to you, I guarantee. And when you read it, pay attention to God's promises and His teachings and, whenever applicable, ask God to bless you with the promises and blessings. It will help building your faith and certainty of His promises onto your life. By doing that, hopefully you will see God start to perform miracles in your life in front of your own eyes and heart.

Besides, I also encourage you to pray together with other people. For example, pray with friends, pray with a small group, and even call the prayer line on the phone, or submit your confidential prayer requests online. These are all different ways to encourage your prayers for a miracle.

Of course, it's best to make sure that all information is confidential. It's better to pray with people who do not know the friends whom you are praying for personally, or who are involved, since it's best to make sure all information and matters are kept in professional and confidential manner. For example, if I am praying for one of my students at the college, I would definitely not talk to other teachers about this particular student whom I am praying for because I am then taking a risk of exposing this student's situation to all the people on school campus.

Lastly, do not try to make miracles with your own hands. Do not try to manipulate or control situations. Just go to God, express your thoughts to Him and lay everything into His hands and let go. Let God do His work. He is the God. Let Him to be in charge. It's better to relax with a humble heart, ask Him for more faith for yourself and learn to trust in Him more daily. Believe His sovereignty, His final word, and His decision is best. Whatever the outcome is, whether it is matching your will or your desire, keep praising and thanking Him as God. Be obedient and submissive. Keep trusting and believing He plans the best for you.

Miracles are supposed to be accomplished by God's hands, not human's. Miracles are supposed to be performed when there seems to have no way. How can you have miracles in life? Let God perform the miracles by His power, and not by your own abilities, skills or your hand. Trust in God because we sometimes cannot even trust ourselves.

QUESTIONS TO EXPLORE:

Q. 1 Can you think of a miracle that has happened in your life when it seemed impossible?

Q. 2 How would you recognize miracles when they occur?

Q. 3 What kind of miracles would you like to have in your life now?

CHAPTER FOUR

God's Eye Is On Your Financial Needs

There is a friend any time you can call.
It does not matter where you fall,
A friend who provides, guides, and gives you all.
This friend has everything you and I can call.
He is the greatest and most trusting of all.

Charis Chung

Shortly after I got baptized by the Holy Spirit and officially became a Christian, I had a dream one night. I saw a caterpillar in the dream. Even though caterpillars have never been my favourite insect, the caterpillar I saw in the dream was very special. It had a sparkling body, and when it moved, it looked quite beautiful, like a moving light. Moreover, in the dream, I also heard a little voice say to me: "This is a praying caterpillar. Since you have now become a Christian, you also need to pray like this caterpillar." I believe that was a lesson to me with that dream. Somehow, throughout the years, prayers have becoming a very essential and important activity for me in my daily life. I would also say that through continuous prayers, I could see numerous miracles performed in front of my eyes.

Life is like a walking journey. It is a long process of walking and learning. Prayers are very important in the journey because prayers not only help us to express ourselves, but prayers also draw us closer to God. To express our thoughts and feelings to Him, to worship Him, to praise Him, to confess our sins, to know Him, to learn and understand God, and to listen to His guidance, to follow, to obey, and to be blessed by God Himself. I use all forms of prayers: praising, worshipping, singing, confessing, asking, requesting, reading God's Words (The Bible), sitting still, kneeling down, standing up, walking, or conversational prayers wherever I am. What I've learned is that miracles are always through sincere prayers. Thus, if you want to have miracles happen in your life, you need to learn and spend time in prayers. It is a process. But if we take His hand and walk on the journey with God, never let go. He is trusting, and He is more than willing to teach us, bless us, speak to us, guide us, and help us, regardless of the situations we are in.

The story of $1,400 miracle I shared in Chapter 2 is just one of the miracles I received from God throughout the years. There are other miracles God performed to help me out financially throughout the years. And all I can say is, He is a very caring God. His eye is on our financial needs. If we are in Him, fear Him and keep disciplining ourselves to follow Him, He does extend His helping hand.

Another memorable miracle where God helped me financially happened during that hard summer in 2014, which I've already shared a bit about in the first chapter. This was, the summer when I rented the living room and the sofa bed from a friend in North Vancouver.

After I completed my post graduate studies from University of British Columbia, I quit all my jobs and decided to go away in order to explore the world. When I returned, I had no job, no money, no nothing. I rented the living room and sofa bed for several hundred dollars each month from a friend in North Vancouver. I tried very hard every day to apply to all kinds of jobs all over the city. But it seemed there was a dark force blocking all paths. I insisted not to ask family or friends for financial help, so I just kept telling Jesus every day that I needed money. I continued applying to different jobs, and some employers asked me to submit my University transcripts to them so I ordered them from U.B.C. where I did the Bachelor of Music degree and the Master's of Education degree.

One time, there was only several hundred dollars left in my pocket and I knew I had to pay my rent in about three days to my friend. I also knew very clearly that if I paid my rent, then I would not have money to buy food. The picture was crystal clear to me. I even debated within myself that may be I should hold on to the rent and buy some food first. I kept praying nightly, asking for His counsel: "Jesus, I need money. I only had money to either pay rent or buy food, and I do not know what I should do. Tell me, what should I do? Pay rent? Or hold onto the only money and buy food first? Jesus, I need money." I think even Jesus was a little bit impatient with me. After two days, I still prayed the same prayers and kept on asking Him for advice. Finally, I heard a still small voice said to me: "Give your friend the rent first." I almost wanted to say, "Satan, stay away from me!" But knowing that was the answer I got from the Holy Spirit, I gave the money to my friend for rent two days early. My friend was surprised that I paid her two days earlier than the due date and reminded me I could pay her later. I insisted that that was fine with me. Inside, I said to myself, "You better take it now, or you may never get it." Knowing that I didn't have any more money to buy food, I kept praying to my Lord Jesus and asked for His help desperately.

The next day, on my way to U.B.C. Registrar's Office to pick up my transcripts that I ordered for some job applications, I walked to my bank, to withdraw some money to pay for my transcripts. I knew it would be the last time that month that I could withdraw money. But to my very surprise, I found there was a chunk of money in my account! I was astonished, and I was surprised! All of a sudden, tears kept rolling down my cheeks non-stop. I first realized it must be God answering my prayers, and again and again, I double checked my bank slip. Yes, there was still a chunk of money in my savings account. But who sent me the money? Where was the money come from? Was it from any of my former jobs in the past? Or was there any music schools or radio stations owe me money from the past? I kept asking these questions. It was not a small amount. It was over a thousand dollars. All kinds of questions were on my mind and I started doubting myself. What if the money didn't belong to me? I should not take it! Even though I needed the money, but if it is not my money, I couldn't take it.

After a second thought, I decided to go inside the bank and find out what happened. I told the teller what happened, and kindly asked her to check where the money came from. The teller spent a few minutes on the computer, and confirmed that yes, the money was for me under my name. When I asked about who sent me the money, the lady checked again but told me that she could not find out who sent the money to me. She only said it was deposited to my savings account under my name that morning.

Once again, tears rolled down my cheeks after I stepped out from the bank. I verbally kept thanking and praising God on my way to the Registrar's Office. At the same time, I was still wondering who sent me the money. I thought of my mother, but how could she have sent me the money? Since I came to Canada, she had never sent me any money through the bank. She didn't know how to send me money and she didn't know my bank account information. I also checked the time, and it was in the middle of the night over there in Hong Kong, and I knew she would be sleeping. So I decided to wait until the afternoon and phone her later to find out.

After lunch and I applying for more jobs in the afternoon, I walked down to Waterfront Park in North Vancouver, which is very close to where I lived that time. I spent time with God every afternoon there and I prayed to Him. I also tried to talk to people and see if I could find an opportunity to share His gospel with people at the park. That day, I did the same routine, and around 6pm, I knew it was about 9am in Hong Kong, I called my mom at the park.

My mother picked up the phone.

"Good morning, mom!"

"Good morning!' she replied. Right away, I asked my mom if she had sent me some money.

"Have you received it?" she asked.

49

"Wait, how did you know how to send me money? How did you know my bank account information....? How did you know I needed money...?"

My mom explained to me that long ago one time when I visited home, I had a piece of paper which on it had all my bank information on it, and she saw that one day I threw the paper in the trash can, and she picked it up when I was not home and she kept that piece of paper. She also told me that she thought of my situation and guessed I must be in need of some money, so she took that step to send me some.

I kept thanking her for how much she had helped me at that critical time, and deep inside, I was awed by how God used my mother and made all things happened to help me at that very dark and needy time in my life.

Ask, and it will be given to you;
seek and you will find;
knock, and it will be opened to you.
For everyone who asks receives,
and he who seeks finds,
and to him who knocks it will be opened.

Matthew 7: 7 - 8

I have to say, my mother has always been one of the greatest gifts that God has blessed me with in my life. My father died suddenly when I was seven years old and my mother had a very tough life to raising all six of her children. And throughout the years, my mother had always taken care of us very well through our childhood. She was fair to each one of us, and never really showed favouritism. She never pushed us to learn anything we didn't want to learn. At the same time, she would always encourage us to choose and make our own choices and decisions, not like many of my friends, who told me that their parents always pushed them to do this or that, basically what their parents wanted them to do. My mother always respected us and let us choose whatever we wanted to choose.

One interesting thing is, from elementary school to high school, then to college and university, all my schoolmates, friends, and co-workers who met my mother told me they wished my mom was their mother. Which to me, I was not really surprised. I am very thankful to have the best mom!

I now not only had enough money to eat, but to join the "Get Published Now" writing program. I had a writing project in my heart for over fourteen years that I wanted to start. Before that, writing the book came up onto my mind again for the eighth or ninth time, and I knew I really should seriously think about it again, since during the pandemic, God once again spoke to me about fulfilling this "mission".

I joined a short writing boot camp and I remembered after talking to my coach about the financial needs that I needed to write this book, I kindly asked her to pray for me before we said goodbye after one coaching. I had been waiting for a refund from the government for over a few months. I started to pray for the refund money. That week afterwards, I kept praying to God that if God does me a miracle of getting the money back from the government, then this time, I would be willing to really start writing my book. I made a promise to God that yes, this time, I would not procrastinate again. If I got the money back, I would start writing this book!

I prayed every day about the money. As usual, I prayed sincerely, consistently, and at least a few times a day, just like I used to pray before all the miracles happened throughout the years.

One night, before I went to bed, I spent some time reading the Bible and a few devotional books. Then I prayed to God about the money again. I used my phone to check my bank account balance. Still no money. So I decided to pray one more time before I turned the light off and went to bed. I trusted and believed that if God really wanted me to write this book, He will, again, perform a miracle as He had in the past. I slept well that night.

The next day when I woke up, I didn't know why, but there was a very small voice said, "Check your bank account again." I thought, Again? I just checked it a few hours ago before I slept! But somehow the idea rang in my mind, and because my phone was just next to my bed, I thought, Ok, I will. Unbelievable, the Government had refunded me the money that morning. I was so excited, happy, and thankful! I phoned my high school buddy Suzanne right away, and told her about the miracle God had done for me that morning.

On one hand, I was so excited about the miracle that God had done for me, as I received the money after a few months of waiting, but on the other hand, as a sinner, I started to hesitate on whether it was wise to spend all the money I had and put into this writing project.

Suzanne suggested that it may be wiser to save the money and I totally understood and agreed. For the next while, I started to hesitate, question, and somehow did not want to "give up" the money I received. What if I use the money to buy something that I always wanted to buy? That would be more fun! And at the same time I could also save some up for future use.

All of a sudden, I found there were many many good excuses to not to put the money into the writing project. I really hesitated about my decision because I knew I would be missing the money for sure. So for the next few days, I thought I had sorted out the problem - I would save the money and not register for the writing project. I had made the decision.

Shortly after, I had a bad toothache and so I went for an emergency to see my dentist. I was on antibiotics for ten days, and during that time, I once again had a bit more time to think of what I should do after I got better from that toothache. I realized and confessed to God that I should have done what I had promised Him to start writing the book that had been in my heart for such a long time; the promise that I had made to God again and again. I started to realize that the book was not about me. It was about God. About His miracles. About people. About sharing God's light and hope to people who need His light, hope, comfort and encouragement. It is for anyone and everyone.

Finally, I decided to boldly take the step of writing the book. A step that I knew would be pleasing God. A step that I knew would not be selfish. A step that would be for God and for the others. God has been so good to me. God has saved me through Jesus Christ. God has forgiven all my sins. He also gave me eternal life after death, and a new life on earth here since I accepted Jesus Christ as my Saviour. He has walked with me through all the darkness in life, and He also blessed me with different dreams that have come true.

He has given me so much that I thought I should also give something back to God.

I decided to use the money I got to put into the project that I was called to do. I decided to start writing this book to share about God, my best friend, and His miraculous power and authority. I want to accomplish this mission and vision in my life. I want to testify the truth of God who I know personally, and I also am excited to share His Miracles. I want to share God's glory with people. I also want to share God's power to encourage people and to give some hope in this dark and hopeless world. I want to introduce His light back to this world. I pray that this book can bring some of God's light, hope, love, grace, miracles, and welcome new lives into His kingdom. I also pray that God will use this book to bring encouragement, healing, and comfort into each reader's heart, soul, and mind. I pray this book will bring you a new life. A new life with God, abundant and free. God Bless You, dear friend.

One lesson I learned through this miracle is, when you are willing to give up something for God, He will always bless you. It had been a while I since buying a new phone, and I wanted to renew my iPhone model. Somehow, after I registered into this writing program and started writing my book, at a very good promotion, I got my newest iPhone with a very good promotion. And because of this phone contract, I was offered a free $300 gift card. And with this gift card, I got an instant pot (that my sister Christine always recommended me to get), a very nice backpack, and a new electric kettle. A few months ago before Christmas, I also got myself an air fryer and a beautiful winter coat at surprisingly good prices. And there are more blessings from God. I would never thought I could afford all these luxuries in such a short time. I myself do not know how to explain it because it is also a surprise to me. All I can say is, these are all miracles from God. Or maybe I would say, when I give up something for God and to obey Him, He rewards me in a miraculous ways.

Giving is one of the big lessons we all learn in life. Wherever I serve at different ministries in churches throughout the years, whether in British Hong Kong long ago when I was young, or at different churches in Western world, it is sometimes very hard to find people who give quietly. Especially those who give with humble hearts. I have met people who come to different ministries and right from the start emphasized they want to play the piano in front of the group, in front of the congregations, or sing under the spot light. I have also met wealthy people who come in the group to make a big announcement, handing me an envelope and telling me about giving a big donation of $30 to the group as an offering.

Isn't it comforting to know that God sees everyone as their real self? God does not look at what's on the outside; what position you have at the church; whether you are the director or you are a kitchen helper. God sees everyone in everything. Most importantly, He looks at our hearts, not our faces, talents, or titles.

In the past when God blessed me with enough money, when I knew people who around me needed help or were in a financial crisis, I had given out thousands of dollars to hope to help out in their very difficult time. I did not make an announcement. In fact, I never publicly or intentionally told people. (This is the first time I am sharing this with more than one person.) I did it in secret and with quiet manner because I did not need to brag about how spiritual or how generous I am. Everything is from God, and so are all His blessings. I knew I was just doing something right and pleasing in God's eye.

I would humbly say, if there is one thing that I could kindly suggest here is, regardless of whether you are a believer of God or not, when you give money out to the needy ones, do not brag about it. Do not make it known so loud. It is because God sees everything, including your motivation and your heart. When He is pleased with your kind acts, at the right time, He will reward you Himself.

God's eye is on our needs. Our financial needs, our emotional needs, our spiritual needs, our mental needs, our vocational needs, our physical needs, and our career needs.... When He blesses us with our needs, may we also share our blessings to meet others' needs.

QUESTIONS TO EXPLORE:

Q. 1 Are you facing financial struggles right now? How would you like God to help you?

Q. 2. Do you have all your financial needs met?

Q. 3 If all your financial needs are met, what and how are you going to use it to the others?

CHAPTER FIVE

God's Hand Can Open Doors For You

There is a power beyond all powers,
A God beyond all gods.
This power can open doors where no one can shut,
This God can open windows even
when the doors are shut.
Yet this power came so lowly and humble,
This God came so powerful thus
we need to be humble.
Have faith in this power,
And have faith in this God.
Then the power in you,
Will reflect the God and the power of God.

Charis Chung

Have you ever faced a situation where you feel stuck, with no hope in front of you and no way out behind you? It could be when you've faced a terminal illness, or you've lost a job that you count on, or someone took the promotion at work and you were supposed to be the one who should be promoted. How do you deal with those experiences? Do you go and complain about it, argue about it, or do you turn to God or someone you believe who has a higher power?

Dear friend, if you are facing a similar situation right now, I want to encourage you to know that God knows everything, and He knows what you are facing, the situation you are in, and He wants to help you. He wants to first tell you to not be afraid, and not to worry. He sees everything that is happening and He understands your pain, and the way you feel helpless. "Come to Me", He says, "I will give you my peace and rest, which is beyond what this world can give." The God that I know understands every tear you drop, every suffering and pain you have encountered. Have faith in His Comfort and tell Him how you feel, what you want, and after you tell Him your feelings, your worries, your anxiety, and the very unfair situation you face, then leave all things into His hands, as He will judge and solve the problems and difficulties for you. One thing you need to know though, it may take some time for you to wait. But He will never forget what you have gone through, and what you have told Him. Trust in Him as a child trust her parents. Have faith in Him, as a child has faith in her teacher. Believe in Him, as a child believes in the school principal. There is someone who is wiser, who knows everything, who sees everything, and who will judge everything in the end. Have faith!

If you say you do not have faith or cannot trust, just ask. Ask God to give you faith. Ask Him to help you to believe in Him. Ask Him to help your disbelief, and you will notice, gradually, that your faith will grow. It will grow like a little seed, if you water it every day, give it a little bit sunshine daily, or may be bless it, talk to it, sing to it, pray for it. And in the end, you will see it sprout. You will see new life come out of it, as it grows slowly every day. It is a miracle. A miracle that no one can push, no one can manipulate, no one can change, and no one can control. Only God can. Yes, He is the God who can part the sea into a dry land, He is the God who can make a way when there seems to be no way in or out, He is the God who does not need anyone to give Him power because He has all the power. Trust in Him and learn to have faith in Him. This is a great weapon we can use any time when we are facing injustice, unfair situations, or oppression. He can push the dark force away and open a new way for you to step in.

Moreover, when His light is in you, and when you are abiding in Him, you can walk boldly with His light, and your path, for sure, will become brighter. Have faith and trust Him. And do not forget to turn to Him whenever you face a difficult situation. Again, turn to Him, speak to Him, pray to Him, express yourself to Him and ask Him what you want, then leave it into His hands. Then wait and watch.

Here I would like to share with you another miracle God did for me when others were trying hard to slam the door on me. It's a true story that I will never forget but am forever thankful for.

After I finishing the music diploma, I took a year and studying vocal performance with Ms. P. Mailing at the Academy of Music. After that, I auditioned for the music academy's Bachelor's in Music Program. By God's grace, I was offered a full scholarship to finish my degree there. However, after about a month into my program, my mother told me that the family could not support me financially any more. Since I just turned and became a landed immigrant at that time, I was thinking that may be I should go to the school counsellor and asked about how I could borrow student loans from the government to finish my scholarship program instead of quitting it. I was very interested in learning vocal performance and that was also the first year I was exposed to an opera workshop, which is a royal form of art, I believe.

So, I made an appointment to see Mrs. Smith, the school administrator and counsellor for the music students. I sincerely told her I really wanted to do the full scholarship program but since I did not have money to live on, I asked her if she could help me apply for some student loans. Mrs. Smith did not reply in a kind or helpful manner. Instead, in a hostile voice, she said to me, "Charis, What makes you think you can and will become a performer or a professional singer?" How old are you, Charis? Do you know that it is very hard to be a professional performer? What kind of abilities do you think you have?....And how will you pay back the money when you finish school?" She got up from her seat, opened the file cabinet in her office, pulled out a file, and said to me seriously, "This student took piano lessons with us since he was four-years-old, and he is now studying music in New York, and he is doing very well." She stood up again and pulled out another file. "This girl learned violin with us when she was five, and now she is studying at Juilliard." She showed me about five or six students' files, not only confirming that they were all very talented students, but that I would never be a performer."

I didn't say a word. I also didn't have guts to yell at her. I had never had an experience like that. But deep inside, I felt hurt, insulted, and treated poorly and unfairly. Tears kept rolling down my face and I didn't bother to even wipe them as they kept rolling down. I was discouraged, hurt, and depressed. Then Mrs. Smith said to me, "Is there anything else I can help you, Charis?"

"No. Thank you very much," I replied. Then I left her office.

There was only one other person in the office who saw me when I went out. The woman just looked at me, wondering what had happened but she never asking.

I went to the washroom, and cried deeply. I washed my face, then walked to Kitsilano Beach. I looked at the seagulls. Even though it was a beautiful day, my eyes didn't see any beauty. I felt oppressed, insulted, and discouraged by this "counsellor" whose job was supposed to encourage students' studies. I prayed to God about how I felt, and I asked God to comfort me and to help me.

After a long time, I decided to go home.

God blessed me with a little job so I could keep taking voice lessons and the opera workshop at the school even though I quit the full scholar ship program due to financial insufficiency. I was very interested and actually was pretty amazed by what I learned in the opera workshop, having a combination of singing, acting, music, dancing, and costumes. It was such beautiful art form!

I started to love operas. I was also very excited about participating in three performances from the opera "The Marriage of Figaro", in which I was Cherubino and sang one of the famous arias "Voi Che Sapete". I had so much fun rehearsing and I forgot the hurtful experience from the office that day.

I seldom was happy with my own performances, but during those three performances, I felt pretty good. And each night after the performance, there were audience members who came up to me and said very encouraging words. I felt very encouraged, glad, and thankful.

The following Monday after the three nights of performances, I was so excited to find out which operas we were learning next semester, so I went to school early in the morning to check out. I looked at the announcements on the board again and again, back and forth. I saw the lists but my name was not on it. Why? How come? I did a good job in the performances and I still wanted to learn about operas. Why was my name not on it? What happened? Who decided it?

I felt very afraid, worried, and nervous. Who should I talk to? I needed to find out the reasons why my name was not on it.

Mrs. Smith was the only one person who dealt with students, so talking to her was the only chance I had. I went to her office and knocked at her door. I told her honestly that I was very disappointed that my name was not on the list of next year's opera workshop, and I asked why I was cut from the workshop. I asked if there was anything I did wrong. Mrs. Smith calmly said that the school had a meeting after the last performance on Friday and decided that from then on they were not going to use any performers who were not on their full scholarship program. She told me if I really wanted to talk to the music director, I should phone him myself.

I asked for his phone number, went to the pay phone on campus and talked to him on the phone. I told him I was very disappointed, discouraged, and upset that my name was not on the list. I also told him that I heard that I was not allowed to join the opera workshop. I told him I was very interested in learning and performing operas and I asked him if he could allow me to join. Of course, I was more than willing to pay the tuition for the workshop. The music director repeated exactly what Mrs. Smith said about their decision. Then he said to me, "But Charis, if you really want to do operas, I'll keep you in mind. If anything comes up, I'll call you." I nodded, with tears in my eyes. He continued, "But it will be just acting. No singing at all."

I knew that it was useless to talk any more. I felt hopeless. I replied politely, "Yes, David, please remember me, and if an opportunity comes up, please call me any time." I then hung up the phone.

"But it will be just acting. No singing at all..."

That line was repeatedly playing in my mind. I thought, I have never known any opera that includes acting roles without a singing part. Tears kept rolling down my cheeks. I knew it was hopeless. I felt hopeless in learning any more about operas. I felt hopeless, sensing I had no way out. I felt hopeless, like I was being betrayed. How could a music school do such harmful, discouraging thing to a music student, a music lover?

I went to the washroom and I cried. Then I washed my face again. Once again, I walked to the Kitsilano Beach. The weather was nice. I sat on the green grassland, looking at the ocean. The scenery was beautiful, but my heart was very heavy. I had nothing I wanted to say. There were seagulls coming and going, and I also heard some birds singing, as if they were singing a song to comfort me. I sat there for a long time, and I repeated the Lord's Prayer a few times:

Our Father who art in heaven,
Hallowed be thy Name.
Thy Kingdom come,

Thy will be done,
On earth as it is in heaven.
Give us this day our daily bread,
And forgive us our debts,
As we forgive our debtors.
Lead us not into temptation,
But deliver us from evil.
For thine is the kingdom,
The power and the glory,

For ever and ever.
Amen

Even though the prayer itself was comforting. Tears kept flowing down my cheeks. I did not know why the school did not allow me to sing. I thought I had learned well and I had fun together with the others. Although it was my first semester learning about operas, I liked it so much. I wanted to keep learning about it and I also wanted to sing and perform operas.

At that moment, I felt hopeless. Somehow, I also felt betrayed, oppressed, and mistreated, similar to when I was in Mrs. Smith's office. No one could help me, and no one would understand me.

Sitting at the beach by myself, I had no one to turn to except God Himself. I poured my heart out to my God. I told Him that I was very upset and felt very hopeless in the situation. I told Him I love learning operas and I also love singing. I told Him I did not understand why they cut me out from the opera workshop so cruelly, and I also told Him I did not know why the music director told me even if there is an opportunity for me to join again, it would be just acting but no singing at all. I expressed how I felt to God, how much I felt hurt and how there would never be another opportunity for me to learn opera again.

Then I felt the Holy Spirit comfort me by reminding me of some of the miracles that God had done to me - how God healed my final stage of Tuberculosis, how I saw a glimpse of Heaven one dark evening, how He miraculously provided me different jobs. And in the end, I started to pray to God for a miracle. I told God that if He is willing to open a miraculous door for me, I asked Him kindly to do so. I told God that I trust in His power and His miracles. I started to praise God for His love, grace and mercies to me through the years and all the miracles which He had performed to help me, and I also sincerely asked Him to help me out again if He was willing to. I confessed my sins to Him, saying that I was pretty mad at the people at the school, but I asked God to forgive me and I said I would leave everything into God's hands, and whatever the outcome was, I would learn to be happy, obedient and keep trusting and walking with my God. That morning, I said a long prayer to God and then I went home.

About a month and a half after that day, while I was resting at home after dinner one evening, the phone rang. I picked it up and answered it as usual. The woman introduced herself as Joan and said she was calling from the Vancouver Opera Association. I felt a little bit surprised and she told me she phoned me on behalf of Leslie Uyeda, the music director of the association. She explained that Ms. Uyeda would like to invite me to join their chorus and to perform the opera "Turandot" at the Queen Elizabeth Theatre. She then told me about the amount of money that I'd be paid. I was puzzled, and double-checked, asking, "Ok, so that's the amount I have to pay for my tuition?" She laughed and said, "No, that is the amount that the Opera Company is going to pay you to join them." I accepted the offer right away. After I hung up, I started dancing, singing and praising God in the living room. I could not believe what and how God opened the impossible door for me!!! God really surprised me that time!

Prayers invade the impossibilities. It is with prayer that we express our trust in God. With prayer, we pour out what is on our hearts to Him. With prayer, we strengthen our faith. With prayer, God helps us grow our faith. With prayer, we express how we feel to God, what situation we are in, what our difficulties are and what the mountains in front of us are. It is also with prayer that we try to move the mountains. With prayer, we try to ask God to make the impossible to be possible. With prayer, we build our friendship with God. With prayer, we believe that God listens to us. With prayer, we trust God will do something and act for us. With prayer, we trust when we share with Him, and He will do the rest. With prayer, God gives us His peace. With prayer, He gives us His hope. With prayer, He gives us His love. With prayer, He comforts us, strengthens us, empowers us, builds us up, encourages us, helps us, and answers us all according to His will.

Dear Heavenly Father, here I pray for my dear friend

who is reading this book. I believe this is not a coincidence that my friend is reading this book. It is planned by You. I pray that You will bless my friend. It does not matter what situations, difficulties, or mountains that my friend here is facing. I believe in your mighty power. The power that made Jesus Christ be resurrected from his death. With this same power, I pray You will also help my friend here to solve the problems and move the mountains that my friend is facing. I pray for more blessings from You to my friend here. I pray that You will forgive all my friend's sins, iniquities, and things that my friend did wrong in the past. I pray, Heavenly Father, that You will bless my friend with faith and trust in You from now on because You are the only true God in this world. I pray that you will give my friend your peace, your love, your grace and your joy. Help my friend grow in their faith in You. Bless my friend in their daily life. I also ask You to heal my friend. Heal my friend in all different areas of their life - financial, emotional, mental, vocational, spiritual - all areas that my friend needs healing. May your healing power bestow miracles into my friend's life. And this power will stay in my friend's life, from now on until my friend meets You again. In Jesus' name I pray and bless my friend here. Amen. Amen.

God's hand can open doors for you. But God is not a genie. Yes, God has all the power to open any door, but we need to make sure we do not command God to do our will. Instead, after we pray to Him, we leave everything unto Him, trusting and believing that He will plan the best for us. Whether it turns out to be our will or against our will, we should be happy and keep trusting and believing that He answers according to His kindness and judgement. We need to trust and believe that God's wisdom is better than our wisdom and demands.

Are you facing a situation where you want God to open a door for you? I kindly suggest you go to Him, pray to Him, pour out your heart to Him and ask Him to help you, guide you, and bless you according to His will. Then go with peace, faith and trust that God will do the best for you. And be happy regardless of what the outcome is. The more you do this, the stronger your faith will be, and the more you will see things with your spiritual eyes. May God bless you, dear friend.

One thing I would like to share with you, though. God does not always open the doors we ask for Him to open for us. Yes, God can open doors which no one can shut. At the same time, I also have to say that, God sometimes shuts the door. And when He shuts the door, no one can open it. At that time, we have to trust that God has the best reason to shut the door. As said earlier, let God be God. Let Him take control. Trust in Him that if He is the best God, and if He knows the best, He will definitely plan the best for us. Simply trust Him, believe in Him and be obedient to Him.

Lastly, I would like to share with you, dear friend, about a very special and important door. This door has always been open for everyone in this world. Yes, everyone. Anyone. This door holds no boundaries. It is a door of connection, a door of hope, a door of healing, and a door of salvation. Anyone who goes through this door will receive blessings, healing, salvation, and eternal life. Through this door you can see God. Through this door you can know God. Through this door you can communicate with God, and develop a special friendship with God. You can talk to God any time, any where. This door will also lead you to Heaven one day when you leave this earth. Yes, through this door, you can become the child of God, and one day you can meet God face to face in Heaven, and you can live there eternally. This door has been opened for a long time, and may I encourage you, dear friend, to walk into the door.

QUESTIONS TO EXPLORE:

Q. 1 Have you ever experienced as if all doors in front of you are shut? What happened?

Q. 2 When is the last time you experienced a door that was opened for you when you felt disappointed?

Q. 3 Do you believe through the special opened door, you can see and meet with God?

CHAPTER SIX

God Wants To Use You

God wants to use you to bring glory,
Glory that transforms darkness into light.
God wants to use you to bring light,
Light that glorifies His name and His kindness.
God wants to use you and your prayers,
Prayers that give hope and prayers that give life.
God wants to bless you with life,
Life that brings another life in this lost world.
God is light and life,
And only this light can create another new life.

Charis Chung

Since I had quit the full-scholarship music program at the music academy, in order to keep taking my voice lessons and the opera workshop in the first year, I decided to pray and look for a part-time job. One afternoon, I went to the Pacific Centre Mall which was one of my favourite malls in town, and walked around the mall, seeing if there were any opportunities for work. A very beautiful store which sold all different kinds of beautiful and artistic decorations and ornaments caught my eyes. Every thing was so beautiful in the show window. And then I noticed a little sign saying "Hiring a Part-Time Sales Representative". All of a sudden, I had hope in my heart! And so after browsing the shop window for a while, I could tell that I really liked the store, so I decided to go in and talk to someone. I asked for the manager and there she was. I explained to her that I was studying part-time and would like to work part-time to sustain myself. She kindly suggested for me to bring in my resume and so I immediately gave her my resume which I typed up the night before. She took it politely. We had a nice short chat and then I left the store.

I told God many times that I liked the store very much and I also found the manager to be a very nice lady, so I would like to work there. I even told God that I did not have much time to go around and apply to different jobs because I was so busy with my studies at school. My study and music practice schedule was always packed, and I attended church on the weekend, so I couldn't afford to look for jobs that were far from me. I told God that I wanted to work there, and asked God to allow me to bless the store and bless the people I would meet there.

A few days later, I decided to go to the store again and talk to the manager. She seemed to be a bit more interested in me now, and introduced herself as Valerie. She started to talk to me about the hourly rate and responsibilities. I emphasized to her that I decided not to work on Sundays, since I was a Christian and had to attend Church. But I could work all day Saturday and any time during the week days after school. Even though she was a bit disappointed that I didn't work on Sundays, she promised that she would talk to the owner for me.

Another few days later, Valerie phoned me and told me the good news - I was hired! I was very glad, thankful and praised God, especially because they allowed me to have Sundays off.

Do you like shopping? What do you like to shop for? Clothes, shoes, watches, jewelry, or furniture? Or those beautiful decorations and ornaments like the Hummel Figurines, the David Winter Cottages, or those limited editions of plates and collectables by different artists? I love those decorations and ornaments which I would see every day in the store!

All the beautiful art work, the crystal figurines, Hummel figurines, Lilliput Lane Collectable Cottages, Jackson's decoys, glass paper weights, B.C. jade jewelries, Department 56 Christmas Villages. I felt like going shopping every time I went in to work. Valerie was also one of the best people I've ever met! She not only had a beautiful face, blonde hair and big blue eyes, but she also had a very kind and gentle heart.

Valerie and I used to work together on the same shift most of the time, and so we started to know each other better and became friends. We talked about everything. She told me she liked classical music very much and I told her I liked the ornaments in the store. She told me stories about her son and his family, and I told her about my mom and my family. She told me I was her best salesperson in the store, and I told her she was the best manager ever! She shared details about her family, and I shared details about my God. Working with Valerie was fun and time went by faster every shift.

Since I did not have much experience in sales at that time, Valerie was a little bit concerned of how well I could perform. For me, I like to help people, and I also liked the products we sold, and so I thought if people would come in, I would just try my best to help out. I trusted that God would do the rest for me.

And in my second week of my work, God was very nice to perform a miracle for me.

Valerie, another girl Lina and I were working on the same shift. Somehow Valerie went out to the mall, and so it was only Lina and I left inside the store. Lina was standing very close by the door and I was standing at the far end corner, so we could keep an eye on all corners of the store. That morning was quiet and no one had come into the store yet. Finally, a man came in with a baby in the baby cart. He was dressed a bit shabby and he also looked a bit shabby. He was wearing jeans and also looked like he had not washed his hair for about two months. And the baby did not dress or look the brightest, either. Honestly, that man did not "look" rich, and judging outwardly by appearance, as if he had stepped into a wrong store.

When they came in, Lina was right by them, but she did not say good morning or hi to him at all. Instead, I saw her looking at that man from head to toe about three times. I started to feel a bit uncomfortable about how impolite she was to him. I started to feel bad as a sales representative, I thought it was our responsibility to show courtesy and to help anyone who came in, regardless of if there was any sale made.

So after giving the man about three minutes to browse around, I walked up to him and said good morning, chatted with him a little bit, and told him let me know if there was anything I could help. I felt better afterwards because at least I knew I had done my part. He nodded with a smile, and continued to walk around the store browsing. After about five minutes, he came back to me and said he would like to get something. I was very happy to help out. In the end, we found out he was actually getting many things! And the things he bought were expensive, too. The whole store was all of a sudden very busy and everyone was working very hard packing, boxing, and checking stock. In that one sale I made that morning, he spent over $4200!

We were all very happy with that big surprise that morning. And especially Valerie. She was very happy and told me once again that I was her best salesperson. And the morning after the man left with his baby, Valerie even went out and got me a muffin as appreciation of my good job.

In retrospect, I am thankful that God gave me the right heart to view and respect people because they are with God's images, not according to worldly judgement.

**Do not judge according to appearance,
But judge with righteous judgment.**

John 7:24

Another reason I liked that job was because we worked together like a little family. There were about eight of us in total. Valerie was our very kind leader, and there were two older married women, then the rest of us were students. We all worked together as a team, and we did care about one another's lives. I remember when I had my first solo recital years ago, they all came and supported me. Basically, we shared lives with one another every day we worked.

One day, Valerie was very happy and told us that she was going to have a baby grandson. All the staff in the store were very happy to hear about the great news. We were counting the days before the baby boy came. We talked about what we were going to buy the baby boy for the shower, and how were we going to plan the party. Everyone was so excited!

Finally, the day came. The baby boy was born in a hospital in Victoria, British Columbia where Valerie's son and his family live. We were all excited when Valerie came in for work because we were waiting to hear about the new born baby! However; that day, Valerie came in with a sad face. She didn't say a single word as she walked in, and we all wondered what had happened.

One hour, then two hours passed by and Valerie was still quiet in the store. I even wondered if I had done anything wrong. Everyone was quiet but we knew that we were there for one another. Gradually, each person went home after their shifts until only

Valerie and I were left.

I wondered what I should say or not to say, but I was glad that at least I was there for Valerie. I knew that there must be something wrong. At last, Valerie started to talk to me when there was no customer in the store.

Valerie told me when her grandson was born, he was born with a medical condition sent the baby to the ICU and was being monitored. In fact, the condition was potentially dangerous and the baby might die. While talking about it, I saw tears in Valerie's eyes, and I felt terrible about the situation and I also felt helpless that I could not do anything about it or for Valerie.

But my God can! I thought.

I started to comfort Valerie, telling her there was no need to be upset. I told her that only God could help, and I told her I believed God would help! I told her that when things seem impossible, God could make things become possible. I also promised Valerie that I would be praying for her baby grandson every day.

And I did. I prayed for Valerie's grandson just like I prayed for my baby birdies. I prayed every day, persistently, sincerely and repeatedly. I asked God to save this beautiful baby boy. I told God that Valerie was my favourite manager and my best friend at that time. I told God that I needed His help and I acknowledged that I believed He was the only one who could help in the situation. I believed His power, His mercies, and His love and care for Valerie and for her grandson. I prayed that God would perform a special miracle for Valerie and her family so she will believe also in God, who was the Creator of this world and the Creator of Valerie and her baby grandson. The more I prayed, the more I felt God would extend His love and mercies to Valerie and her family.

I checked in on Valerie every day I saw her in the store, and for the first week, nothing really improved. But I knew everything takes time, and praying and waiting on God is one of the most important lessons I've learned throughout my friendship with God. I've heard once that we are living in a "microwave" generation, but our God is a "Crockpot" God. He sometimes does things slower than we expect, but He is never late. Prayers invade the impossibilities and I knew I needed to keep praying, praising, trusting, and believing. And I believed that, if my prayers could match God's will, He would do another miracle for me, for Valerie and for her grandson. By holding onto the promises of God, and remembering that Valerie told me the doctor said if nothing change in the baby's condition, he might be die in a few weeks, I earnestly prayed for the baby daily. I said long prayers and short prayers. I prayed in the morning, in the afternoon, and in the evening. I prayed earnestly and sincerely.

God answered my prayers after about three and a half weeks. Praise the Lord! That day, Valerie came in with a very big smile on her face. She walked even faster than the other days. We all greeted her and could not wait to hear what had happened. After she settled down in the store, she called me to go to the back storage room to meet her, and surprisingly, she told me that there was a miracle that happened to her grandson. The doctor said the baby suddenly was much better, and he would leave the I.C.U. He would stay in the hospital for few more days to be monitored, but if he kept improving, he could go home soon. I was so very happy and surprised to hear the good news directly from Valerie. And I thanked and praised God for what He had done for all of us in the store.

After working with Valerie at the store for about four years while I was studying at a music college, Valerie told us that she decided to take an early retirement, and would be leaving us in about a month. Afterwards, she planned to move to Victoria, B.C., where her son's family was and where she could also see her grandson more often. On the one hand, I was very happy for her, but on the other hand, I felt sad that Valerie was leaving us.

We planned a very nice farewell dinner party for Valerie in Downtown Vancouver, at one of the fine dining restaurants in one evening. That night, we prepared Valerie a good present, a beautiful card, a bunch of beautiful flowers, and we all enjoyed some great laughter, great food, and a great time at the party.

However, fun and great times are always short, and the farewell time came. We shed a few tears when it was time to say goodbye to Valerie after the dinner. Valerie told me to stay behind after the dinner because she said she had something she wanted to talk to me about. Watching her saying thank you and farewell to everyone, I was even wondering if I broke something in the store on accident. May be she would ask me to pay for it.

Finally my time came, and Valerie came to me with her beautiful big smile and said, "Charis, I want to say thank you to you. I want to say that, since you came to the store and worked for us, you have been sharing your God with me. At first, I did not want to hear about your God because I used to believe in this same God. But since I was divorced from my husband, I went through a very hard and unhappy time, and I said to myself and to God that I will never trust Him again. But when my grandson was born with that serious medical condition in the hospital, where he was facing death, you said your God would heal my grandson and you also said you would pray for him every day. Then when I saw the miracle happen, I gradually and slowly looked for God and I went back to Him. I confessed my sins and I accepted Jesus Christ again in my life. Gradually, I feel much happier, and now I am living much happier than I was before. I want to give you a compliment and I want to thank you for doing this."

All of a sudden, I didn't know how to respond, I didn't even know what to say. I was so surprised, thankful, and happy for Valerie! We gave each other a big hug, and that was the last time I saw her.

Valerie moved to Victoria as she planned. We still kept in touch with each other through writing and phone calls. But after about one year of moving, sadly enough, Valerie was diagnosed with cancer, and another year later, she died in the hospital in Victoria, B.C. one summer.

I know Valerie is now living happily in Heaven. A beautiful Heaven that God has prepared for all His children who trust in Him. And in Heaven, there are no tears because there is no sadness, no sickness, and no death. Valerie is for sure one of my best friends, and I miss our friendship. However, I am sure, one day, when it is my time to leave this earth, I will be seeing Valerie again in Heaven. Her big smile, beautiful blonde hair, and her big blue eyes. I'll see it all again.

Let not your heart be troubled;
You believe in God, believe also in Me.
In My Father's house are many mansions;
If it were not so, I would have told you.
I go to prepare a place for you.

And if I go and prepare a place for you,
I will come again and receive you to Myself;
That where I am, there you may be also.
And where I go you know,
And the way you know.

John 14: 1 - 4

I'm very glad and thankful that God used me to bring kindness to the man who came into the store in my second week of work. I'm also very thankful that God used me to bring His hope to Valerie's grandson. Most importantly, I'm very thankful that God also used me to encourage and bring Valerie back to Him. I started to realize and learn that life is just not about yourself. Instead, it's about how God uses us to bless others. How God uses us to bring His hope, love, peace, and even His salvation to others.

Dear friend, do you know that life is not about yourself? That's right, life is not about yourself. It doesn't mean that we shouldn't enjoy life or we shouldn't take care of ourselves. Rather, we need to take good care of ourselves first, making sure that we are healthy and, free of sin. We must eat well so we can have healthy bodies to also take care of the others. If we are healthy, we can work and serve God, people, and communities with our skills and work every day. We have to do well in our jobs. It is not to please our bosses or to beat others so we can be promoted. It is to be responsible to God, who gives us the job. When we are with God, God is pleased with us. Be loyal, honest and obedient in little things, and when God sees us doing well, He will then use us more. When God use us, it not only bless us, but also to bless others.

Here I would also like to share with you, dear friend, things that I have learned about how I or we can prepare ourselves to be used by God to bless others:

1. **Purify yourself.**
2. **Simplify your schedule.**
3. **Exercise your faith.**

1. **Purify yourself:** This is the first and most important part. In order to pass God's grace and love to others, there has to have no interruptions between God and ourselves. Imagine there is a drinking straw between God and ourselves. This straw has to be clean, with no substance inside which would block any water that goes through, so the water (God's grace and miracles) can go through the straw easily and smoothly from one side to the other. **Sin** always blocks us from seeing and reaching God face to face. We need to get rid of all sins in our lives in order to reach God. All hatred, jealousy, selfishness, lack of forgiveness, or impatience not only blocks us from reaching God; it also blocks us from reaching others. Thus, confessing our sins, getting rid of all sins in our lives and preparing and cleaning our hearts and spirits should be one of the most important activities we should do every day in our daily lives. Taking away all the junk in our heart and in our minds, and preparing ourselves to have a clean heart and spirit to go to God makes our prayers more pleasing and effective in our lives.

I like to say The Lord's Prayer followed by my confession to God regularly. I confess things I've done wrong in life. I confess things that are on my

mind or in my heart which are not pleasing to God.
I say sorry for the "dissonance" in my life that blocks
my friendship with God. I also ask God to forgive
me even for the things that I do wrong but I may
not realize. I also evaluate myself and my living
regularly. I ask God for His forgiveness and I "clean"
myself spiritually in front of God and to make sure
I am a good "vessel" that God can use before I pray
for the others.

2. **Simplify your schedule:** I think one of the
difficulties or problems we have to deal with now
is that we are dealing with too many things in our
every day life. For example, I have some younger
students who have such intensive daily schedules
that sometimes they come in to my music studio with
their hair wet because they just had their swimming
lessons prior to their singing lessons. And sometimes
they say they have to leave five minutes earlier
because they are running to their maths tutoring
after the music lessons. The list can go on and on.
Nowadays, parents tend to train their children to
become a superman or a superwoman. And some
parents whom I teach also have the same issues they
are often running around to arrange their children's
activities, sports and extra tutoring outside schools.

I believe that not until we quiet down, sit still
and spend time with God, we cannot find quiet time,
confess our sins, communicate with God to improve
our own life and pray earnestly for others. I know
some people keep running around, here and there,
doing this and doing that, doing many chores and

never stop. There has to be a balance. I try to keep myself living a very simple life.

Having a routine is great. For example, since I have two pet birds at home. Every morning, after changing the food, water, and cleaning the bird cage, I then have breakfast. I listen to Dr. Rick Warren's Daily Hope Radio and Dr. David Jeremiah's Turning Point Radio programs while I do the morning duties. I sometimes pray at the time while listening to the ministries. After breakfast, I sometimes will go for a prayer walk, then read the Bible and some devotional books, at the same time, writing down my devotional journal. Then I would have to prepare lesson plans or doing some administrative work for my students at the college.

After lunch, occasionally, I will go to my backyard and take a prayer walk or do a little bit exercise. Then I may phone a friend or two to have a chit chat on the phone and talk about any thing. Singing praises and listening to some beautiful hymns also calms my heart and I like doing that. In fact, my two beautiful canaries Mira and Angel also love listening to music! Sometimes I meet friends for lunches or dinners. Then for the rest of the time I would be busy preparing lesson plans, teaching, doing groceries, laundry, cleaning just like every one of you.

Basically, I keep my life very simple and my mind very clear, giving my heart some rests so I can focus. Focusing on important things and set our priorities are very important. If I have some special prayer items in my heart, I make sure I pray earnestly, regularly and persistently. Thus, simplifying your life and schedule is a must to prepare yourself to be used by God.

3. **Exercise your faith:** The Bible says if we have faith, we can even move mountains. Also by faith, we can invade the impossible. How can we have faith? One of the most effective ways is to hear God's words or read God's words. The stronger faith we have, the more we can accomplish in the "missions" God has for us, and the stronger the faith, the more God can use us.

Like I mentioned earlier, I enjoy listening to all different Christian Radio programs. I also like listening and watching different series by some of my favourite pastors. I like reading devotional books, I like the Bible, and I also like watching or listening to some extra programs that can help me to live better and healthier. For example, a few years ago, God told me He wanted to heal me in many different areas of my life. But I had no clue how? God miraculously told me one night to register for Dr. Jimmy Evan's "21 Day Inner Healing" program. Since then, I have been doing this program plus the next "21 Day Total Healing" program through these years.

To exercise our faith to God, we can also think back and thank God for each past miracle that God has done for us. Name them one by one with a thankful heart. Praise Him for His mighty power and for His grace and mercy to us. The more we see and remember His miracles to us, the stronger we build up our faith in worshipping our God. The stronger the faith we have inside us, the more power we have when we pray. And when our prayers are strong, God can use us to change people, change situations, change environments, and even change the spiritual realm. With our powerful prayers, God conquers for us in the spiritual realm.

Would you like to bring power to the other people's lives? Then start purifying yourself, simplifying your life and your schedule, and exercising your faith in God. Pray to Him often, anywhere and everywhere. Also make sure you believe and trust in God. Trust that He can and will answer your prayers, to your benefit, and according to His will. And do not forget to spend time developing your knowledge, your understanding and your love for God Himself. Read the Bible, listen to His words often, read other good devotional books, watch different sermons on internet and Youtube and I guarantee you that, you will find that God will not only change your life, but He will also use you to change the others' lives.

Life is short. We all have to face our death one day. No one can be excused. Do you want to go to Heaven where there are no tears and you will be happy being with God for eternity? I sincerely invite you to learn how to know and accept God. And when you become one of His children, He not only will bless you, but will also use you to bless the others on earth. We are made for eternity, not just for a short while. May you find your eternal purpose and be used by God Himself.

Charis Chung

QUESTIONS TO EXPLORE:

1. Have you ever had an experience that you felt you are a blessing to others?

2. Was there a difficult situation that you wish you could have helped bring blessings to the others?

3. Are you willing to learn to purify yourself, simply your life and schedule, and exercise your faith? How?

CHAPTER SEVEN

God's Eye Is On Your Body

Only one life, we all have to go.
Only one life, you and I know,
We all have to go.
I surely know where I go,
To the Promised Land I go.
Do you know where you go?
When that day will come,
I will see the glory of the place I go,
And I wish to take you where I go.
Life is short. Time is running out.
Would you like to go where I go?

That place is not far away.
Receive Him into your heart right away.
By God's Grace,
You can also go where I will go.
Then you will also wish,
To take as many friends as you can hold.

Charis Chung

Think back when you were a student, did you enjoy writing examinations? Or when you've gone to a job interview or taken a test for a job, do you enjoy doing those skills tests? Though sometimes I don't like the process, or how the professors facilitate those tests and examinations, I honestly don't mind. As a music and ESL educator myself, I do believe tests, quizzes, examinations, whatever you call them, are valuable and necessary to evaluate how students learn, to see their progress and to evaluate their learning outcomes. And in order to make sure students are capable to jump up to the next higher level of learning, we sometimes have to pass one test to move up, to make sure they have the proper skills learned well. In other words, tests are supposed to be beneficial to the students, rather than block them from their learning.

And life is a test. We are all facing different tests and examinations almost every day. One day you may face a difficult financial situation, the next day you may end up quarrelling with a friend. May be Monday is the worst day for you to get up and go to work because there's a new week in front of you. Or Friday may be challenging for you to go to work since you are already exhausted on Wednesday, and you feel Friday is like the Saturday or Sunday.

Think back the most challenging tests or difficulties you faced in your life in the past, what are the situations? And how did you overcome and solve the tests? Have you ever faced death in your life?

I have. A few times. Yes, a few times. However, I don't think I have enough time and space to share all my experiences about facing death in this book. But in this chapter, I will share with you the first time I faced death.

It happened many years ago. After I finished high school, I went straight into the Vancouver Community College Music Diploma Program. I felt very fortunate at first because I had very little background in music and was basically learning music from scratch. I still remember in the enrolment audition, when the Music Department Head hesitated and questioned me about my background, but my voice instructor, Dr. Jacob Hamm, immediately interrupted and said that even though I had only just taken a few voice lessons with him, I had picked it up very fast.

When in the end I got accepted into the program as an international student, far away from my home in British, Hong Kong, I thought my dream had just started and all things would go well.

However, one night while I was having dinner at home, and I noticed a big lump under my ear. The first doctor I visited told me it wasn't cancer or Tuberculosis even before taking any further examinations or X-rays. Then when my friend Iris suggested me to go to see an acupuncturist, I ran away so fast when I saw the big needles the acupuncturist was trying to attempt on me. I had never seen such big and long needles in my life before! In the end, when the college pianist Ms. Carol suggested that I go see her family doctor immediately, I was told that I couldn't escape a biopsy surgery. The day after I heard that from the doctor, I felt afraid, helpless, and very uncomfortable with the surgery coming up.

There was an extraordinary thing and experience that happened a few nights before that biopsy surgery which I will share later. But here, I'd like to share what happened miraculously after the biopsy surgery that I was found to have the final stage of Tuberculosis.

The Vancouver General Hospital suggested I see the doctor shortly after the biopsy surgery. When I went in the first day, the doctor directed me to take some X-rays. With a total of about twenty something X-rays, I felt the disease I had was definitely abnormal. I had to go through different machines that I have never seen in my life before. I had to stand up, sit down, lie down. At one point, I thought it was like working out in a gym with different equipment. After twenty something X-rays were done, I was sent home without meeting the doctor. And I was told I would need to go back in about three weeks.

After about three weeks, I went into the hospital again and had my second doctor's appointment. I was first told to take another set of X-rays. Yes, twenty something X-rays again. I felt as if I were an expert by that time. After that, I was then sent to meet the doctor the first time after these tests. Surprisingly, when I met him, his first question was: "Charis, would you mind if I send you to go with the nurse again, and do another set of X-rays?" Whaaaat? I couldn't believe it. But I had to say "I don't mind at all." So, off I went to complete another twenty something X-rays on the same day. A total of three sets of X-rays in two appointments.

Finally, I sat down in the doctor's office. He was busy looking at all the X-rays, comparing, murmuring, and kept saying: "I don't understand this, I don't understand this, I don't understand this." I was thinking "If you are the Doctor and you don't understand this, how can I, the patient, understand this at all?" In the end, he turned on the lights on his desk, and showed me the three sets of X-rays which

I took three weeks ago and the two sets from that day. He showed and explained to me that the first set which I took three weeks ago showed that there was a shaded area on my lung, and inside that shaded area, there was a clear little circle, which indicated I was in the final stage of Tuberculosis and it was incurable.

No medicine can heal that final stage of the disease.

Then the doctor showed me the two other sets of X-rays which I took on that same day, right before I met him in his office, and indicated to me that there was also a shaded area on my lung, but in these two new sets, there was *no* circle inside the shaded area. He explained to me that in this case, it could be curable, and he could put me onto the medication. And he asked if it would be okay if he put me on medication for nine months. I said, "It's all fine." (Clearly knew that I had no choice.)

Deep in my heart, I realized that God had mercy on me. And it was God who kept my life. That day, the doctor also warned me, even after the nine-month medication, when I was completely healed, the shaded area on my lung would always be there for the rest of my life. I sadly responded that I understood.

Mercifully, all by God's grace, God did two miracles for me: He not only made the Tuberculosis curable, but He kept my life from the final stage of the disease. After I was completely healed after the nine-month medication, the shaded area on my lung was completely gone. That is also why I passed the medical check-up and examinations years later when my family applied to become landed immigrants in Canada.

God's miracles have always been amazing. And I thank God for all He did for me. Praise God!

"Heaven is a real place.
The more we know about it,
The more we should anticipate it.
As I have often suggested,
Heaven is a prepared place
For prepared people."

Don Piper

In my Father's house are many rooms;
If it were not so,
I would have told you.
I am going there to prepare a place for you.
And if I go and prepare a place for you,
I will come back and take you to be with me
That you also may be where I am.

John 14:2 - 3

Our bodies are fragile. Our bodies are not eternal. There is a higher body in ourselves. When our physical bodies leave this earth one day, the eternal body, the spirit, will go somewhere that day. For eternity. Do you know where you will be going? No one knows when we will be leaving this earth. No one knows when the date is. But that date may come early. It may come suddenly. Are you prepared? Are you prepared to go where your spirit will be going eternally?

Different people from different religions may tell you different places where they will go after life on earth. I have to honestly share, my dear friend, that my relationship and friendship with God of this universe tells me there is a Heaven. A place where God has prepared for all His children. One day, on that date, when we close our eyes on earth, we will open our eyes in Heaven, a place God prepared for all His children, where we will meet God face to face. Heaven is a very beautiful place where there is no sin, no tears, no hatred. It is a perfect place where we meet our perfect Heavenly Father and all our brothers and sisters. And that Heaven is our eternal home when we accept this God of the universe.

I have read many books about Heaven: David Jeremiah's *Discover Paradise*, Todd Burpo's *Heaven is for Real*, Don Piper's *Heaven is Real*, Mahesh Chavada's *Only Love Can Make a Miracle*. I also have watched interviews and testimonies of different people who died and had been to Heaven and came back and talked about their experience. Some of them were not even Christians when they died. However, when they came back, many of them became Christians and some even quit their jobs to become full-time ministers and pastors, sharing the Gospel around the world.

The most extraordinary experience I had about Heaven was the time after the doctor told me I had to have that biopsy surgery the first year of music school. As I said earlier, I was afraid, felt helpless and uncomfortable to have been told that the surgery was compulsory.

It was about one week before the biopsy surgery. I had an "out-of-body" experience one evening when I was lying on my bed and was ready to rest and sleep.

Since I had that big lump on my neck during that time, my body easily felt tired. And I also lost my appetite. I remember that was the first time I did not feel like eating even I was looking at some of my favourite food. Every day I just had the energy to go to school and learn music at the music school, mainly because I enjoyed it. After school, if there were no rehearsals, I would usually go home early, quickly do the homework, have my dinner then rest.

During that time, I rented a basement suite with a working lady who usually came home late and left home early in the morning. In a way I felt good about it because I had no energy to spend additional time to talk to her and socialize. I didn't know the lady myself. We just shared the two-bedroom suite and shared the rent.

One evening, as usual, I finished my dinner around seven o'clock. After showering, I decided to rest early that evening.

My bedroom was dark and I was lying down flat on my bed. My face was staring at the ceiling. My hands rested on both sides. I started to think of the biopsy I was to have next week, then all of a sudden I felt very exhausted and I was falling asleep.

In the last split second right before I fell asleep, all of a sudden, I felt something very strange - I couldn't move my body. Not even my fingers. My eyes were closed, but I felt my body become stiff suddenly, I could not move at all. I tried to move my fingers but I couldn't. I couldn't even open my eyes. I right away asked myself inside my head: What's happening?

Then immediately, my body went to another place. I know it sounds unbelievable, but I am not kidding here. And I knew very clearly I was in another place. I didn't even know what happened to me, so may be it is also unfair for me to explain, but I'll try to explain here.

I first saw a very beautiful green grassland. I mean, the most beautiful green grassland that I had never seen in my life! Have you ever been to Prince Edward Island, the home of Anne of Green Gables? I have been there once with my sister Christine. The green grassland there was the most beautiful green grassland I could find on earth. But the beautiful green grassland that I saw that night was hundred times more beautiful than the one on Prince Edward Island. And on the grass, I could even see sparkling lights like little diamonds among the grass. And there was warmth, little yellow light shining on the grassland. The grassland moved a little bit with the mild wind. The beauty was very hard for me to describe, but I could never forgot. I was so happy and glad to see what I saw. I felt like I was in Heaven.

Then suddenly I felt my body was like an angel - I flew up very high and I was up on the high top ceiling of a big dome. Like those big, church cathedral dome in the shape of a hemisphere. I was on the very top, and I saw there were many angels with white gowns and wings circling around the big cathedral underneath me. I looked downwards to see them. The angels were not walking. They were flying or floating around as if they had no feet. They were very beautiful. And I was above those angels.

Then at last, I heard very beautiful and magnificent music from there! I had never heard such beautiful music on earth before! I have been studying music at music colleges and university for over fifteen years, and in my training, I have listened to all kinds of music - symphonies, operas, oratorios, jazz, rock and roll, concertos, ensembles, choral music, solo pieces, piano, flute, vocal - I can guarantee you, the music on earth couldn't compare to the most beautiful music I heard that night there! It warmed my heart and brought me happiness. Even though I did not see my God's face to face there that night, I could feel that God was with me that night in that whole extraordinary, out-of-body experience, indeed. I was awed by what I saw, where I went, and what I heard in that amazing, out-of-body experience!

The grassland, the angels, and the beautiful music pleased my heart so much and I felt immensely happy. Then I started to smile, and when my lips started moving, I came back to my dark bedroom all of a sudden.

My eyes were still closed. My body was still lying flat on my bed. I felt very strange and I was a bit amazed, a bit surprised, and a bit shocked.

What happened just now? Where was I? I was afraid to open my eyes at first, so I tried to move my fingers first. And yes, they moved this time. Then I slowly opened my eyes and I saw nothing was changed in my bedroom. My brain told myself: I just had an out-of-body experience, and I saw a glimpse of Heaven. Even though I did not see God Himself face to face, I felt very strongly that I was with God. I was so happy and I felt so much love from God Himself. I then asked God in my heart, "What happened? And what is the lesson for me, God?"

Right away, I heard the Holy Spirit speak to me in a small voice: "Just now when you were on the top of that big dome ceiling, where you saw the Angels, and you heard the beautiful music? This world is like the same man-made building. Living in it sometimes can be very hard, and you could get hurt... and it could also be pretty painful. But if you are with Me, you will find happiness and joy. Try to love this world and its people again."

I immediately told God in my heart that I would learn and try. And honestly, up to this day, I am still learning with the help of The Holy Spirit.

Throughout years, I've realized that God not only cares for my visible body, He also cares for my invisible body. And *dear friend*, I can honestly share with you that God also cares very much about your visible and invisible body, just like He cares for me. You may wonder, what does it mean?

Visible body is the body we can see physically. It is our physically bodies. God cares about the health and wellness of our eyes, our ears, our blood vessels, our feet, our teeth, our nose, our neck, our bones, our muscles, our heart, our lungs, our hands, our nails, our hair. He wants us to have healthy body and healthy bones and healthy legs, so we can live healthily and happily.

The invisible body is the body we cannot see with our eyes. It includes our will, our emotions, our mind, our intellect, and most importantly, our spirit. The visible body and invisible body are inter-related and they affect each other closely. Do you remember a time when you've been hurt, and you were so upset that you wouldn't even want to go to work or go to school? You probably felt sick, so you called into the office or the school to cancel that working day or your lesson. I'm sure you will clearly understand the rest I want to explain here.

God cares about both our visible and invisible bodies.

A few years ago, God led me to a healing journey. Yes, a healing journey on my invisible body. God wanted to heal me emotionally, mentally, in my mind, in my soul, and in my spirit. While I was watching a sermon by Dr. and Pastor Jimmy Evans, one of my favourite Bible scholars, an advertisement popped up on the screen about a twenty-one-day inner healing program taught by this same pastor. Somehow I quickly jotted it down in my note book.

About two days later while I was trying to sleep at night, the Holy Spirit told me to register for the program. I replied in my mind: I'm sleeping now. So I tried to sleep.

But that voice said again: "Go and register for the program."

I replied again: I'm tired, and I'm trying to sleep.

That still small voice said a third time: "Register for the program."

At that point, I knew it must have been the Holy Spirit. So I got up, turned my light on, looked for my note book, checked on the web site about the program and I registered that night.

That program helped me so much on understanding, knowing, acknowledging, changing and correcting myself. It was one of the best programs I've ever taken. Shortly before I completed that program, I was hoping there is another program, and there was! The second program was planned a few days after my wish and I was so surprised! I immediately took it, too. I first had no clue on how can I to be healed, where could I find good resources, who are the great people I could learn from, and God guided me step-by-step by opening doors for me. Today, I'm still learning and walking on this healing journey.

Everyone of us has been wounded, hurt and damaged in one way or the other. I know I have been. How do you deal with your wounds and pain throughout these years? Would you like to have a "clean up" in both of your visible and invisible body? I am much healthier and happier than I was few years ago, and I'd love to share with you how you also can be healed by God in just few simple steps:

1. Keep moving and pick up a new sport or interest.
2. Cut down on all sugar, junk food and eat well.
3. Keep developing your friendship with God and with good people.
4. Keep equipping and improving yourself.

1. ***Keep moving and pick up a new sport or interest:*** If you like walking or dancing, keep doing it. Get fresh air and spend time in nature, refreshing your soul and mind. Watching birds and looking for bugs among flowers can release your stress and give you new insights. Believe me. If it has been a long time since you have not learned something new, this is the time! Find something that you like, or you possibly like, go and learn it. It will help you re-focus on your goal and refresh your heart.

   I never really learned how to cycle when I was younger. But I just bought an inexpensive bike just a month ago and I decided to learn it in my backyard. Since I'm not a teenager, of course it takes courage, more energy and more time to learn. But so far, I enjoy it very much, and I enjoy when I try every time. I've learned by watching Youtube and I am improving. I enjoy my bike and it's good exercise.

2. ***Cut down on sugar, junk food and eat well:*** I'm not telling you not to eat ice-cream or chocolate for the rest of your life. I'm also not telling you that you can't eat chips or fried chicken wings. But choose wisely. I enjoy no sugar chocolate and no sugar ice-cream. They are still sweet. And instead of potato chips, may be change to rice crackers or other healthier snacks. They are yummy, too. Again, do not eat them every day. We have to have a control what we eat every day. Also try to eat two or three kinds of fruits daily. Drinking green juice or berry juice is also very good way to cleanse our body. Try to eat clean and eat well. Organic food is better because they have fewer chemicals. I suggest you to go to some whole food stores and find some good vitamins which suit yourself. Many years ago God told me this through a little book I bought from a Christian bookstore. At the time, I could only find one or two whole food stores in town. Since then, I've been seeing them blooming all over the place and the world.

3. ***Keep developing your friendship with God and with good people:*** The more we spend time with God, the more our soul, our mind, our heart, our spirit will be refreshed and renewed, and the healthier and happier we will be. Reading good devotional books also help us live a healthier life. Words are very powerful. Not only what we say, but also what we read. Register for some good courses

also stimulate us not only cognitively, but also spiritually and mentally. I just registered for a free ten-week online class at my church on prayer. We started our first class this Sunday morning and I enjoyed it very much. Without realizing, joining this kind of classes can help develop our friendship with God and with people. But here I want to say, not just believers are good people. Many non-believers are very good people, too. I like to make friends with all honest, kind, and nice people. Having good friends make our lives become healthier and happier.

4. ***Keep equipping and improving yourself:*** There are only two ways of living, either progressing or regressing. If we are not going forward, we are going backward. We need to evaluate ourselves often in all we do, how we are doing, what we should do and how we can improve. Each one of us has our own challenges and difficulties we face in life. How we face and solve our challenges and difficulties is very important. As I heard before, there are only two kinds of people, one who admits the problems and ignore them, and one who admits the problems and find ways to deal with it. And if we also want to live a healthier and happier life, we have to keep equipping and improving ourselves.

We have to acknowledge our problems and difficult issues. Admit that we are weak and need help. Admit that we cannot solve all problems. Admit that we have no power to conquer our own weakness and we need to ask God to use His power to help us. Go to him and ask Him for His help. If you need to take a course or to talk to a helper or a counsellor, do it. Sometimes people who are trained and have the knowledge to help us can open our eyes and give us good suggestions so we can have deeper understanding on our own issues. In order to improve our lives, we need to keep learning, equipping and improving ourselves.

I have known God for many years. I walked through fire and hell with this God of the universe. He never let me go. Instead, He never failed me. It doesn't matter where I was on the journey, He keeps walking with me. I know God not only wants me to have a healthy body, but also a healthy spirit and soul.

Whether you need a physical healing, or a spiritual, mental, emotional healing, come to God, He has the power, the love, and grace to carry you through, *dear friend*.

QUESTIONS TO EXPLORE:

Q. 1 Have you faced any serious illness before? What happened?

Q. 2 If you have faced death before, how did you overcome it?

Q. 3 How can you improve your visible and invisible physical body?

CHAPTER EIGHT

The Finale

Life is a journey where you have no choice
of when and where to start.
Even when you have a choice on the path,
You have no clue which choice
will guarantee a wide and easy road.
The longer you walk on this journey,
The more you may be confused
by your own choice and will.
Someday, you may find your own choice
could lead to a dead end.

Do not be afraid.
There is a higher power, higher wisdom,
and a higher voice.
If you hear this still, small voice and follow,
This voice will lead you to a graceland,
your destiny, and your purpose.
And it does not matter where
you turn on this journey,
This power, wisdom, and gentle small voice,

Will bless you and heal you whenever you need.
This spirit also has a mighty hand,
Which can carry you through fire and hell,
And lead you to the eternal home -
To Heaven.

Charis Chung

Dear Friend,

Let me first sincerely *thank you* for taking your precious time to read my book. This book which has been in the bottom of my heart for over fourteen years, ever since I was healed from the final stage of tuberculosis.

If it takes you three hours to finish reading this book, I sincerely thank you for these three hours that you've spent with me. Time is precious. Every minute counts. Moreover, I do feel honoured that I could spend these three hours with you through this little journey. Thank you.

We may have never met in person, but I would like to say that we still have a chance to meet one day in the Heaven, a place that God has prepared for all those who believe and accept Himself. I certainly am waiting for the day that we can meet in that glorious place, so I can welcome and hug you myself.

I have been praying alone and with some friends - that this book will be a blessing, an encouragement, and a testimony to everyone who reads it. I also have been trusting the light, the hope, and the true stories I've share here will also bring a glimpse of light to you if you are going through a difficult time yourself. No one is an island. If you would like to also share with me about your stories or difficulties, please feel free to write me and introduce yourself. You can find out how you could write me at the end of this book. I would love to hear from you, especially if this book has encouraged you!

If by God's grace, you also would like to know God, or would like to accept Him as your God and Saviour, then please let me humbly suggest you to say the following prayer sincerely and accept Him into your life. Or, if you had known God in your life before, but you have walked far away from Him for a while, and after reading this book, you would like to go back to Him and join His family again like my supervisor and friend Valerie, you can also say this sincere prayer:

Dear God, I thank You for Your love to me.
Thank You for sending Your Son
Jesus to come and save me.
I believe Jesus died on the cross for my sins.
I ask sincerely that You forgive all my sins.
I ask that You give me a new life.
I want to have a friendship and
relationship with You.
I invite Jesus Christ to come into my heart.

I ask that You will be my Lord and God.
Please help me to live for you God.
In Jesus' name I pray.
Amen.

If you have said the prayer above, I congratulate you in becoming a new member, a son or a daughter, in God's kingdom! I now encourage you to find an evangelical church to attend, so you won't be walking on this journey by yourself alone. Instead, you will start knowing other brothers and sisters in this international kingdom. I am sure you will find joy and peace to meet some new friends there!

One thing I will warn you about, though. Becoming a child of God does not mean everything will go well after you accepted God. It also doesn't mean from now on you won't face any difficulties. As you can see from the stories I've shared in this book, we all go through hardships, difficulties, tough times, and disappointments. The point is to walk through those tough times with God's mighty hands, and go through those difficulties with His love and grace. Always continue trusting and believing in Him while you are walking through your journey. You will find those difficulties will lead you to grow and become more mature in your life journey.

Transformation is one of the most important elements in life. A person without good changes in life is like a new born baby who never grow up. It is not about how we were born; it is about how we grow up and keep changing, improving and correcting ourselves on our journey. At the same time, I believe, maturing our character so that we can be more like Christ and God Himself is certainly one of the big "projects" God intends for us to learn, grow and imitate here on earth.

What I have shared in these eight chapters are just some of the miracles God has done in my life through some of the years. There are many more other supernatural miracles which I have not shared in this book yet. For example, God also healed my heart condition one time without any medication. One day when the company I worked for decided to close their office here in Vancouver and move to

California, I lost my job and felt helpless. I cried, standing at the corner of a street. After a sincere prayer with Sabina on the phone, and with my own cries to God on a street in North Vancouver, God miraculously gave me a full-time job in just two hours.

Years ago, while I was living in hopelessness, great disappointment and some sort of depression, when I thought of finishing my life and committing suicide, God stopped me from attempting. God has also blessed me with jobs that I have never applied for, and has also miraculously blessed me with a beautiful apartment suite supernaturally. God has also used me to heal some people's sickness miraculously. All of these miracles occurred because God's power is unlimited and when we have faith and trust in Him, all things are possible.

In retrospect, I admit that I have grown and learned so much after all the hardships, incidents and miracles that I have experienced and shared in this book. If you also would like to know this God who created this world and who also created you, or if you have already said the above prayer with me, but do not know how to start your journey with God, here I would like to sincerely suggest a few things that you could start learning about:

1. To know and love God your Creator.
2. To embrace God and become a child of God.
3. To learn to grow more mature,
in order to be like God.
4. To learn to serve God and other people.
5. To find your dreams, your
vision and your mission.

1. ***To know and love God your Creator:*** No one is an accident in this world. We are all born with a reason and with a purpose. And to find the reason and the purpose, we have to find and know the One who created and made us. Only the One who created you know why He created you, what are you here for, and the best qualities and the uniqueness inside you. To reach our full potential, we have to go back and ask the One who made us because the Creator knows us better than we know ourselves. Without knowing Him, we won't know ourselves better. The God of this universe created you and He loves you dearly. He created you because He loves you. He likes to see you, hear from you, talk with you, do things together with you, enjoy time and laughters with you, help you when you are struggling, deliver you from evil, encourage you when you are discouraged. If there is such loving God who wants the best for you, don't you also want to know Him and love Him? There is a very well-known book named *The Purpose Driven Life* by Dr. Rick Warren. I highly recommend you to read this. It's one of the bestselling nonfiction books in history, selling more than 35 million copies, and has been translated into more than seventy different languages. It will definitely help you to know yourself and God very well.

2. ***To embrace God and become a child of God:*** To know God is not enough. Once you find your Heavenly Father, it is also good for you to return to the family you are originally from God's family in Heaven - where we belong to each other. Where you will meet all of your other brothers and sisters in the family. We all need to connect with one another

and share life, food, and fun with one another. It is definitely not good to be alone or be isolated by yourself. When you know God and also accept Him into your heart and life, make sure you also join God's family-the church, where all brothers and sisters are sharing, learning, growing and encouraging each other.

Here I also need to warn you, just like any other communities, even in churches, you will always find folks who you don't naturally bond well with, or others you may not admire all the time. The point is not to spend the same amount of time with everyone and neglect your own preferences or choices, but to find those who you trust and can build friendships with. A friendship that builds each other up, encourages each other and supports each other.

At the same time, try to also learn to love the unloving people because church is full of broken people, too. Try your best to stay peaceful at all times. Here, I would like to suggest the Alpha Course offered by different churches around the world. Anglican priest and author Nicky Gumbel is the founder and developer of the Alpha Course. This is a ten to twelve-week course which usually starts with a very nice meal together, a video clip of about ten to fifteen minutes, and a table discussion. Anyone including non-believers are all welcome to join this course, and whether you are a new comer to the church, or a person looking for some new friends, all are welcome to join this unique and fun program!

3. ***To learn to grow more mature, in order to be like God:*** Unless you are dead, all lives grow. Either grow older, taller, heavier, wiser, or more mature. Once we accept a new life in God, we are supposed to grow each day, and grow to be more like our Heavenly Father. Life is a classroom, and we need to keep learning, understanding, growing and changing into a better and a more mature version of ourselves, more like our God. No one likes to stay in kindergarten for the rest of his or her life. Everyone needs to be changed into a better way each day, each week, each month, and each year. We need to learn about God and learn to be more like Him. We need to improve ourselves in love, joy, peace, patience, kindness and self-control, making sure we are developed in our lives as we are growing every day.

How do we grow? I would humbly say, the simple and first steps are to read God's word the Bible and talk to Him daily through prayers. Spending twenty or thirty minutes a day to read God's words and pray to Him will for sure help you to grow in Him, rewarded by His blessings and grace. I've done that for many years and this is one thing I can guarantee you, dear friend. Go to a bookstore and get a Bible. Read the books of Genesis (about how God created this world) and read the Gospels (the books of Matthew, Mark, Luke and John) so you can learn and understand about God's plan of saving all people on earth. Also read the Proverbs and Psalms which can give you God's wisdom to live on earth and introduce you to beautiful poems. These books from the Bible, for sure, will help you to grow healthily, happily, and wisely in God's family. If you are a visual person and learn better in watching, it may be helpful to get the Gospel movies like *The Gospel of John* or *The Passion of the Christ.*

4. *To learn to serve God and other people:* As we all know, we are all different. Everyone is very unique in this world. Even inside the same family, all siblings are different from one another. No one is the same as the other. God is a God of varieties and he does not clone people or animals. Each person's finger print is different, and no one shares the same fingerprint. Our talents, abilities, interests and skills are all different. But each one of us has his or her own talents and abilities that others may not have. Have you ever asked why do we have natural talents and skills and abilities that the others may not have? There must have a purpose, and I believe the purpose is to use that unique talent, unique skill, and unique ability to serve God, serve others, serve the community and serve this world properly so those abilities won't be wasted. A beautiful song sung by someone who's talented in singing will probably touch your heart much more than the song sung by someone who's tone deaf. A delicious meal cooked by someone who is talented in cooking will probably impressed you and make you happier than a meal that is cooked by someone who doesn't know how to cook at all.

We all are part of this world and we all have our part to this world. Each of us has his or her part to serve, to contribute, to influence, and to impact the world in a better way and in a higher way. This world also needs all different talents, skills and abilities to make this world into a better place. Are you willing to use your God-given talents, skills and abilities... to make this world to become more beautiful, enjoyable, and encouraging? I encourage you to join different groups, communities and churches to find out, learn and develop your innate, God-given talents and abilities to make a positive impact to this world. Do not forget, you need this world, and this world also needs you.

5. **To find your dreams, your vision and your mission:** Are you hanging on to a job that you are not interested in at all but to just get the good pay cheque each month? Are you just staying in the position in order to get the benefits and a retirement plan? Or are you choosing a specific career because your parents want you to be in? Dear friend, I'm afraid you may be wasting your time or even wasting your life. I have gone through those years myself. Sometimes, we need to think twice. Dear friend, evaluate your life and find out what your natural talents, your interests, your abilities, the desires of your heart are. Ask yourself what would you like to do to make contributions to your community and to the world. Ask yourself what would you like to learn or accomplish in the next ten years or so. Ask yourself what would you like to develop in your skills, knowledge, understanding, or abilities. All your answers may lead you to a surprising door which bring happiness and wellness to yourself and to the world you are living in. And most importantly, ask and pray to God of this what He wants you to do.What are His visions and missions He has for you? The more you know what you are supposed to

do in His kingdom, the more you know the purpose He has for your life, and if you follow and obey, the more meaningful your life is going to be.

Dear friend, may I sincerely wish you a great and wonderful journey in front of you!

If you have been a follower of Christ for a long time, and you also have been spending these three hours reading this book, let me also sincerely *thank you* for reading! Your interest and kindness is already an encouragement to me. Even though your life journey may not be as dramatic as mine, let me also share with you something that may also encourage you in return. Especially when challenges or troubles come your way, I hope the following lessons I have learned will also give you some lights on your path:

1. Turn to God whenever you have a concern or face a difficult time.
2. Make sure to pray sincerely and consistently when you face any challenges.
3. Do your best and leave the rest to God, trusting in Him.
4. Keep praising God, regardless of what happens.
5. Believe and trust that God is your perfect Father regardless of the results.

1. ***Turn to God whenever you have a concern or face a difficult time:*** Try not to talk to your boyfriend, girlfriend, your husband or your wife right away when you have a concern that comes up. Also try not to phone your best friend immediately

when you are facing a difficult challenge. Instead, talk to God just for one minute anytime, anywhere, and in any way. His power is greater than anyone else, and bigger than all your family members or your best friends. Our God never sleeps or slumbers. It is actually faster to talk to Him than to anyone else. Furthermore, instead of worrying about it yourself or getting more and more anxious when you are alone, talk to Him, and He can give you His peace right away because He is the Prince of Peace. Afterwards, consulting with family and friends of course will bless you more.

2. ***Make sure to pray sincerely and persistently when you face any challenges:*** Learn conversational prayers. These are prayers that you pray in a simple, short way, anywhere and at any time, just like a conversation. It is because sometimes it makes it harder for us to pray if we can only pray when we can kneel down, find a quiet place, or when no one is around. Many challenging situations and difficulties come at the time we have no time to look for a quiet place to kneel down and pray. Since our God is everywhere, anywhere, pray while you're lining up to pay at the cashiers, pray when you're waiting at the bus stop, pray even when you are at your job interview. Make prayers be flexible and adjustable. And of course, if you are praying for some big issues, or something important, make sure to spend more time in different places, to pray sincerely and persistently. Then God will see your sincere heart and desire, and will answer you according to His final will.

3. ***Do your best and leave the rest to God, trusting in Him:*** We need to be responsible to do our job to the best of our abilities, as if God is watching us. We should do our best to please God and show Him we are doing it to please Him, not other people. Then the next step is to believe that God is our perfect Father. If He wants us to have whatever we ask, He will give it to us. But if He does not want us to have what we ask, learn to be obedient and still be happy. Make sure to leave the rest unto God's hands. Do not manipulate God. Do not try to control God or anyone. Learn to "leave it". Let go and let God take control. I know this lesson is not easy because we tend to control and use our hands to make things happen, but there is no need to. I learned that only people with an "orphan" spirit like to "make things happen". Please remember that we are not orphans. We are children of God. He is our Father. He will give us the best. There is no need to manipulate or control.

4. ***Keep praising God, regardless of what happens:*** I once experienced a very tough time, for over five years of my life. I called it a "desert time". It seemed nothing went well at all during those years. I lost everything. I applied for almost a hundred jobs but nothing came up. I had different accidents during those years. It seemed bad things came up one after the other, nonstop. I have friends who saw me struggle through those years and even they could not understand.

In the end, one thing I learned was that I kept saying "Praise the Lord! Praise the Lord! Praise the

Lord!" out loud when I face anything bad. These words would not only stop me from feeling totally discouraged and depressed, but I could feel myself pushing back the dark force. Just remember, it does not matter how difficult the time is, it will one day be over. Continuing to praise God not only comforts your heart and soul, but also change the atmosphere in the spiritual realm. Keep praising and keep asking God to help you whenever, wherever. He will help you.

5. ***Believe and trust that God is your perfect Father, regardless of the results:*** If you got sick and you went to see your family doctor, and he checks on you and told you that you've got Pneumonia and he put you on antibiotics for ten days, would you follow his instructions? Do you love the taste, smell, and colours of the antibiotics? You probably don't. Why do you still follow the doctor's instructions and take the medication on time, on the requested amount carefully and obediently? It's because you trust your doctor. You trust that your body will be changed for the better. You trust that even though the medication is bitter, it smells bad, it is not attractive, it is still good for you. It helps your situation, your body, and your soul, you can finally function much better. At the end of the medication, you can enjoy life again.

I sometimes think life's challenges and difficulties are somehow similar. We may not understand why we get them, but if we get them, we better face them with a positive mind, go to our "life doctor" our God and listen to His words. Be patient and obedient, listen and read His words a few times a day. Keep on doing it for at least ten days, then you will probably see there is a way out. His words and kindness will change your mind, your soul, your body, then your behaviour, your thinking and your life. God can heal us in every area of our lives so at the end our character and our hearts will be changed. Our characters and our personalities will also be changed into better ways.

It is always hard to say goodbye to family and friends because we never know when will be the next time to meet again in the future. Furthermore; before we say goodbye here, I would like to end with an interesting miracle just happened this week.

His Eye Is On The Sparrow, the title of this book, has been in my heart for over fourteen years, ever since I started to have the idea of writing this book to share about God's miracles in my life. I have always hoped to use it as my book title. However, when I finally started writing this book, different friends have suggested different names for the book, and I also found they are all great ideas. So, I stopped thinking of using this old idea from fourteen years ago. Just the past week, I had been struggling about which title to use, and worries and anxieties came along the way as I also found out there were already a few books with the same title. I remember fourteen years ago when I Googled the same title, it was not as common. I started to worry a little bit.

But about ten days ago, when I found that I could still use the same title for my book, I couldn't help to thank and praise God for this special title. Surprisingly, on that same morning, when I came back to my living room, a little sparrow flew into my suite! This beautiful little sparrow was lost. He was flying here and there and even hurt himself. I tried my best to save him, and found out he was a very beautiful, strong little sparrow! I blessed him, took a picture

tᵉ Charis Chung

of him with my phone and released him. This little sparrow flew away quickly, stood on a tree, and looked at me for about two or three seconds, then he flew away. It was such a very special day and moment for me. In the bottom of my heart, I felt God had confirmed this book title. I was amazed and thankful for this little miracle of confirmation.

His eye is, indeed, on the sparrow. It does not matter how others look at us, or whether we find ourselves important or not, we all have a very precious value to the God who created us. To Him, we are worth a million times more than a little sparrow. If He cares so much about a little sparrow, what makes you feel He does not care about you?

May God open your eyes so you can see Him with your spiritual eyes. May God open your ears so you can hear His gentle voice. May God open your heart to receive and accept His love for you. May God open your arms so He can embrace you with His arms, His grace, His mercies, and His love daily.

His eye is on the sparrow.
And His eye is on you.
God bless you, dear friend!

Sincerely,
Charis

118

ABOUT THE AUTHOR

Charis@hiseyeisonthesparrow.com

Charis Chung is a professional performing artist, singer, musician, specialized in Western Art Song and Opera. Charis is also a certified music and ESL Instructor. She is also a member of the Canadian Actors' Equity, signed in by the Vancouver Opera Association. Charis was born in British, Hong Kong. She came to Canada as International Student and have been residing in British Columbia for many years where she calls her 'earthly home'.

Charis's performances have been broadcasted through CBC Radio and Television throughout Canada. She was the Provincial Senior Voice Competition Representative in 1997, and she made her Live Interview Debut with CBC Radio on topic about Western Art Song & Opera. Charis has won numerous awards and scholarships in competitions, music schools and camps.

Charis is also a dedicated musician, music and language educator with passion, mission and vision. She has extensive teaching experience in the public sector, community centres, different music and language schools and academies. Her students have been accepted into various music college and universities, have been finalists of the Miami Jazz Festival, and have traveled around the world, singing in major concert halls, museums and parliaments.

Writing this book has been in Charis's heart for over fourteen years. Since she was miraculously healed when she was facing the final stage of Tuberculosis (T.B.) that even the doctor could not understand. In retrospect, Charis thinks her life is as dramatic as an opera itself. She has faced death a few times, lost her jobs, lost her place to stay, lost everything....

Charis believes miracles happen to people who have a pure heart, a childlike faith and who insist on asking. In this inspirational memoir, Charis shares true miracles she experienced first hand in her life.

Printed in the United States
by Baker & Taylor Publisher Services